CIN·CIN

ANDREW RICHARDSON

With contributions from **LEWIS BIRCH** AND **SHANE TAYLOR**

Text by **JIM TOBLER** With a foreword by **FRANCIS MALLMANN**

Figure.1
Vancouver / Berkeley

Cataloguing data available from Library and Archives Canada

ISBN 978-1-927958-74-2 (hbk.)

Book design and prop styling by Natalie Olsen
Editing by Marial Shea
Copy editing by Grace Yaginuma
Indexing by Iva Cheung
Photography by Kevin Clark
Images on pages 6 and 8 by Desy Cheng
Printed and bound in China by C&C Offset Printing Co., Ltd.
Distributed in the U.S. by Publishers Group West

Figure 1 Publishing Inc.
Vancouver BC Canada
www.figure1pub.com

CONTENTS

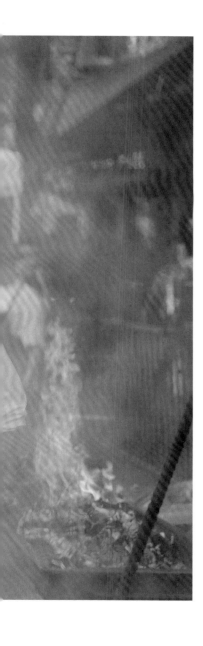

FOREWORD

It was in September of 2014 that I flew to Vancouver to cook with Andrew Richardson at the wonderful CinCin Ristorante. Working at the restaurant with my team, and recreating our fires on Robson Street, was certainly a huge honour. We cooked with the best produce of Vancouver, produce that arrives every morning— crisp, fresh and bright—at the doorsteps of this temple of grace.

Silence during the battle of restaurant service is a precious gift. And when I say *silence*, I mean it. Everything Andrew does is done with a gentle, quiet embrace, a silence that fills the restaurant with a vivid, but calming, spirit. A kitchen that delivers food as delicious as CinCin's is is certainly not a cathedral of hush, with the clanging of pots and pans and voices calling out orders. But—when you see this skilful man walking his kitchen peacefully but in haste, you feel the true romance of his passion, and his deep commitment to simple perfection.

The only way to cook simple food, besides the knowledge of our craft, is to make sure our most important ingredient is always respect. That is what I found on the palms of Andrew's hands. That is what I felt in the silent grace of CinCin. ───────────────

Francis Mallmann
chef, author of *Mallmann on Fire* and *Seven Fires*

For over twenty-five years, a winding stone stairway has been transporting diners from the frenetic bustle of Vancouver's Robson Street to an intimate dining experience at CinCin Ristorante. While CinCin enjoys a reputation as an Italian restaurant, it is more accurately described as "Italian-inspired." Italians like to say there is no such thing as a truly Italian restaurant outside of Italy. This may well be true, yet each day executive chef Andrew Richardson and his dedicated staff reinvent such essentially Italian dishes as risotto and branzino, making them quintessentially CinCin.

What, after all, is Italian food? Is it buffalo mozzarella? Water buffalo are not indigenous to Italy—they were brought from Asia. Tomatoes? Believed by many to be the ultimate Italian ingredient, tomatoes were brought from South America; initially, Italians thought them to be poisonous. So where do we draw the line? Perhaps there's no need for a strict line at all!

We could borrow the analogy of how an Italian might cook when visiting Canada. Instead of reproducing the exact dishes they prepare in Italy, they may well adapt techniques and ingredients to their host country. A cook can be driven by a time and place, and Andrew is more than familiar with this methodology of ingredient matching. If a product similar to one in Italy is available, then a matching cooking technique is used. If the season dictates a Pacific Northwest product, appropriate techniques are applied to that.

Andrew remembers his first few months at CinCin. "I took stock of everything," he recalls. "To have the restaurant giving guests what I wanted to give them, at a consistently high level, without any pretension, meant we had to go from scratch, from the ground up." He bases his cooking on what he considers the most vital principles of Italian food. First and foremost, he allows seasonality to drive the menu. At heart, his approach is simple, with not too much technique (which is more a hallmark of French cooking). He selects the freshest ingredients and invites their natural flavours to sing.

Andrew spent nearly two years creating the dining experience he knew in his heart was right for CinCin's guests: a raucous rusticity balanced by the refinements and flourishes diners have the right to expect—not for the sake of being fancy, but to fully express the components on the plate. His philosophy, and his practical passion, is to create food that is honest and easy to understand, yet ultimately elevated into meals worthy of what the Michelin guide would call a "destination" dining room.

Many CinCin recipes spring from his love of all things Italian. An example is his passion for prosciutto, which was sparked by a visit to Italy to see a friend. This friend took him to a restaurant near the Pantheon in Rome, where he was amazed by the sight of prosciutto hanging from the rafters. Buffalo mozzarella is another ingredient Andrew considers a natural. Defining versatility, it has a rich, creamy softness that pairs well with acidity and citrus (think tomatoes and lemon) or, alternatively, with pickled vegetables (such as beets) and crostini, their crunch contrasting with the soft texture of the cheese.

He was reluctant to include grilled romaine; after all, it's dated and it's everywhere. Yet, who can deny how delicious it is, especially when seasoned, dressed with olive oil and grilled over burning wood. "We give it that little something extra," says Andrew, "allowing it to show what made it so great in the first place."

La minestra is a classic vegetable soup. While its method is routine, the ingredients change with the seasons—perhaps parsnips, celery root and carrots in winter and then green beans, English peas and fava beans in summer.

Polenta and risotto are two other essential staples. Three types of polenta meal are used, including coarse and fine. Sometimes CinCin uses instant polenta, a great alternative if you don't have time to stir a pot for an hour. The *peposo* pasta dish (see page 80) was inspired by an excess of sauce from braising the ribs. Used first for a staff meal, it found its way onto the menu.

In many ways, the food at CinCin is grounded in a respect for nature and her fragile bounties. An example is how the smoked sablefish risotto was inspired by the kitchen's commitment to minimizing waste. This dish not only puts the sablefish trim to good use, it gives a distinctly Canadian twist to an Italian staple. And speaking of fish and sustainability, all the fish served at CinCin (and other Toptable Group restaurants) is part of the Vancouver Aquarium's Ocean Wise program. This guarantees that a fish is an ocean-friendly variety harvested in season.

Diners are also assured of a true farm-to-table meal, with regionally sourced meat and produce. Offering a plate with something other than fresh ingredients is basically unheard of at CinCin. Needless to say, Andrew is a regular at the local farmers' markets. On Wednesday, Thursday, Saturday and Sunday in spring, summer and fall (and Saturdays during winter), he's checking out the stalls to see what might add a flavourful flourish to the evening's menu. Fresh herbs perhaps, or purple fingerling potatoes, or sometimes nothing at all—but he is there every week. Favourite suppliers deliver their best directly to the restaurant's back door, from tomatoes and mushrooms to nasturtium flowers with their lovely black pepper flavour that finishes with a vivid shot of fresh honey.

CORONATION
(ALMOST)
SEEDLESS.
WAKE UP
YOUR
TASTEBUDS
3.00/lb

A typical day in the CinCin kitchen begins around 10 a.m., when pastry chef Lewis Birch puts bread and buns on to bake for the evening's service and decides what pastries to make. On wood delivery days, another staff member will be on hand to accept and stack it. One cord of savoury wood—a mixture of birch, apple and alder—arrives, and it is a labour of love to get it into the wood room, up the stairs from the rear delivery entrance. Fresh laundry, wine, you name it, there is a constant ebb and flow for Andrew, restaurant director Richard Luxton and the entire team to monitor, inventory and store. By 2 p.m., the kitchen is infused with aromas of fresh bread and baking. More cooks arrive to do preparation and to begin the process of lighting the fiery heart of CinCin: the spectacular Grillworks Infierno.

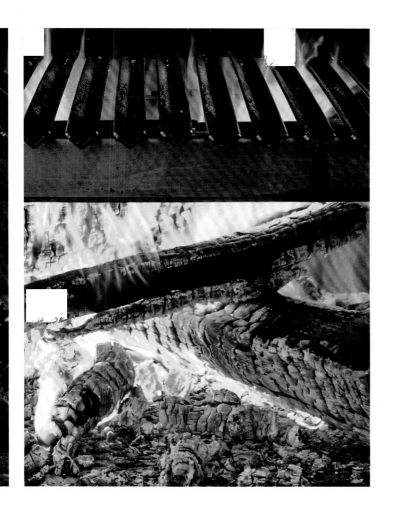

This superb piece of contemporary machinery and technology, facing the main dining room for all guests to see, has one foot planted firmly in the Neanderthal age, when fire was an element of community, sustenance and survival. Through the metaphysical equivalent of what the Australians might call a walkabout, Andrew found a kind of soulmate in the Grillworks. He expresses it best when he says that "sometimes people want to have a meal that touches the basics of fire and flavour, coming right off the land they live on." That's exactly what he offers at CinCin, every day. "The Grillworks wood-burning oven is fundamental to this process. We use every bit of it, right down to the ashes."

Wood has a special place at CinCin, augmented by long-lasting and clean-burning fruit-wood charcoal. Birch, apple and alder woods top the list, each imparting their own unique character to the flames and, of course, to the smoke.

Andrew discovered a kindred spirit in Francis Mallmann, a world-renowned authority on cooking with fire. Mallmann's two restaurants in Argentina are soulful and extraordinary (imagine an eighteenth-century feast with a modern wine list). His cooking style is brilliantly captured in his second cookbook, *Mallmann on Fire*. In 2014, Mallmann paid his first visit to British Columbia, bringing his signature "gaucho grilling" to CinCin. In collaboration with Andrew and the CinCin team, Mallmann devised a fire and spit right on Robson Street and mesmerized passers-by with the aroma of two-inch-thick rib-eye steaks cooking for over eight hours. Mallmann's mantra is "Food is not feeding the body only, but feeding the soul." Andrew was galvanized by what he calls Mallmann's "primal" approach to cooking.

Back in the CinCin kitchen, 'round 3 p.m., a particularly savoury form of "team building" is getting underway. A few large plates and bowls full of food start to appear on the kitchen "pass." Most assuredly not on the menu, these might include polenta fried in chicken fat, or green beans, kale and red peppers. Or you might find octopus stir-fry, curried chicken or honeyed chicken wings. Preparation is shared by staff, and service is help yourself. This is the daily staff meal, and it's a time when staff can sit down together and talk about aspects of the kitchen, daily menu changes, how busy the evening appears to be—all overtop a running commentary on the food before them. "Sometimes we take away an idea for a possible future menu item," Andrew says. "But mainly, we enjoy sharing a few moments together before service begins."

Another opportunity to gather and exchange ideas is the Saturday staff meeting. At the height of the 2015 tomato season, Andrew brought in a bowl of locally grown heirloom San Marzano tomatoes, to be featured on the menu with a serving of basil and mozzarella di bufala as well as being the key ingredient in a bolognese sauce. "These are amazing," he says, "as if they came from Italy half an hour ago. They have relatively low seed content, with high pulp, so they have an incredible sweetness to them. The bolognese is fantastic."

Wine director Shane Taylor goes over two new wines being poured by the glass as of that day, and Richard Luxton summarizes the evening's outlook: "We have 160 reservations, and expect roughly eighty walk-ins. So, as usual, we will be quite busy." Everyone disperses and the action begins.

Acclaimed bar manager David Wolowidnyk helms the CinCin bar. He was making artisanal from-scratch drinks at West for years before it became *de rigueur*. "What I make in house here is determined to a large degree by the restaurant itself," he says. While he insists that he would "never use the word *experiment*," he does work closely with staff to study what guests are looking for. He is consistently creating new and exciting levels of hand-crafted cocktails while staying true to CinCin's elegant yet approachable style of high-level comfort food.

The same can be said for Shane Taylor, who calls the shots on a wine list that features over one thousand labels. "I think of this restaurant as refining the classics," says Taylor, "a kind of slow growth in progress, rather than a radical change in what diners expect. The wine list reflects that." There are indeed some exotic labels from Piedmont and Tuscany, even Napa and Canada. But the focus is mainly on wines that work well with the cooking, from some great Vermentino and Falanghina through to Chianti Classico and Nero d'Avola.

While standards of service and food are routinely high, there is no such thing as a typical meal at CinCin. When asked his favourite dish, Shane replied, "If it were a death-row last meal, I suppose it would be the saffron risotto and braised shank." He added, "Andrew changes the menu often, not just seasonally, but even daily, so there is always something really exciting for even our regulars to try. Impossible to pick one favourite." Most of the team at CinCin would likely agree.

You could have an evening that starts with rosemary focaccia alongside some spelt buns, all made that morning by Lewis Birch. Alongside, you could enjoy a dish of olive tapenade, nestled in a pool of extra virgin olive oil. Perhaps a glass of Verdicchio and a bottle of mineral water. Creamy burrata from Italy, those San Marzanos absolutely explosive and a chiffonade of vivid basil, all drizzled with olive oil and some freshly ground black pepper. Saffron risotto with gremolata and lemon zest. Chargrilled branzino. Ricotta-filled handmade fresh ravioli with toasted hazelnuts. Different nights, different seasons, a myriad of fresh and fiery choices.

This book is your invitation to share in the CinCin fire and magic, and even bring it to life in your own kitchen. Whether you follow the recipes rigorously or use your imagination to make them your own (which would garner a nod of approval from Andrew), you'll find an unlimited world of flavours to explore and savour.

LIST OF RECIPES

CONTORNI

Braised carrots 151

Sautéed Swiss chard 152

Giant white beans 153

Chickpea purée 154

Fennel-onion confit 155

Eggplant Parmigiana 157

Brussels sprouts 158

Giambotta 159

Garlic, rosemary and
sea salt roast potatoes 160

Whole roasted garlic 163

Gnocchi Romani 164

Polenta alla griglia 165

Polenta, two ways 166

Rosemary and Parmesan
focaccia with olive oil
and tapenade 167
Bread starter
Green olive and garlic confit tapenade

DOLCI

Warm dark chocolate fondant 173
Caramélia gelato

Chocolate mousse 175
Chocolate crema, chocolate sponge cake, dark
chocolate glaze

Maple-roasted apples 178
Brioche, smoked-milk gelato,
brown sugar and vanilla crumble,
toffee sauce

Dulcey panna cotta 182
Vanilla shortbread, blueberry compote

Gelato and sorbetto 184
Vanilla gelato, chocolate gelato, coconut
sorbetto, lemon and mint sorbetto

Grilled peaches with amaretto 187
Caramelized hazelnuts, vanilla mascarpone

Lemon crema with smoked
pistachios 189
Lemon fluid gel, smoked pistachios

Lemon semolina cake 193
Citrus sorbetto, brown sugar and
pine nut crumble

CinCin tiramisù 197
White chocolate sponge, espresso soak,
mascarpone cream, maple and rum sauce

Rhubarb and ginger cannoli 199
Ginger cream, rhubarb compote,
ginger and brown sugar crumble

Vanilla panna cotta 201
Vanilla sugar, strawberry sorbetto, strawberry
and cocoa nib tuiles, strawberries with
balsamic and olive oil

Chocolate truffles 204
Dark chocolate olive oil ganache,
salted butter caramel ganache

Macarons 206
Burnt orange ganache, duck fat
caramel ganache

Petits fours 209
Chocolate marshmallows, pâte de fruits,
pecan and cocoa nib shortbread

BASICS

Soffritto 213

Pickling liquid 213

Risotto base 214

White chicken stock 215

Bouquet garni 215

Reduced brown chicken stock
(succo) 216

Vegetable stock 217

Lamb/duck sauce 218

Mushroom essence 219

Brown butter 219

Salsa verde 220

Basil pesto 220

Basil pistou 221

Salmoriglio 221

Classic vinaigrette 222

Meyer lemon vinaigrette 222

Chili oil 222

Lemon oil 223

Orange oil 223

ANTIPASTI

Calamari are very small, so we finely chop the prawns before they're gently stuffed into the calamari with the mushrooms. For easiest preparation, buy your squid frozen and already cleaned. From Spain, the piquillo pepper is a perfect accompaniment here—not hot, but with a lovely spiciness. If you can't find shishito peppers, you can use red jalapenos.

Fire-grilled stuffed calamari — shishito peppers, arugula and piquillo pepper sauce

SERVES 4

½ cup (125 mL) **Piquillo Pepper Sauce** *overleaf*

Mushroom Prawn Stuffing *overleaf*

2 ½ Tbsp (40 mL) **Classic Vinaigrette** *page 222*

8 **squid tubes and tentacles**
(tubes about 3–4 inches/8–10 cm long)

8 **fresh shishito peppers**

Extra virgin olive oil, for the squid

Sea salt and freshly ground black pepper

4 **handfuls arugula**

Maldon salt, for the arugula

Pimentón (or smoked paprika)

Prepare the piquillo pepper sauce, the mushroom prawn stuffing and the classic vinaigrette.

When the stuffing has cooled, place in a piping bag with a large plain tip.

Fill the squid tubes with the stuffing, being careful not to pack it in too tightly or the stuffing will burst out during cooking. Secure the ends of the squid tubes with cocktail sticks by pushing the sticks through each opening from one side to the other.

Light a wood-fired barbecue, or preheat a gas or charcoal grill or cast-iron grill pan.

Dress the squid tubes and tentacles and the shishito peppers with olive oil, and season with salt and pepper.

Warm the pepper sauce.

Grill the squid and peppers for about 3 minutes until nicely coloured and the peppers are just tender.

Spoon and spread the sauce on 4 plates.

Dress the arugula with the vinaigrette and Maldon salt. Place a handful in the centre of each plate.

Distribute the grilled squid and peppers around the salads, and sprinkle with a pinch of pimentón.

Continued overleaf

WINE NOTE **If you can find it, an Italian Riesling, such as G.D. Vajra Pètracine Riesling 2013 from Piedmont, Italy, would do nicely. Easier to locate would be Tantalus Riesling from the Okanagan valley.**

PIQUILLO PEPPER SAUCE

One 13 oz (375 mL) can piquillo peppers, in liquid

1 ½ Tbsp (22 mL) olive oil

2 large shallots, minced

2 small cloves garlic (or 1 large), minced

2 fresh or dried bay leaves

1 Tbsp (15 mL) granulated sugar

3 Tbsp (45 mL) Manzanilla sherry

½ cup (125 mL) water

Sea salt and freshly ground black pepper, to taste

Drain the piquillo peppers. If they're whole, cut them in half lengthwise to remove the seeds. Cut the peppers into ¼-inch (6 mm) strips.

In a medium frying pan, heat the olive oil. Add the shallots, garlic and bay leaves, and gently cook for about 5 minutes. Season with salt and pepper.

Add the sugar and strips of pepper. Stir well and cook for 5 minutes.

Add the sherry and water. Bring to a boil, lower the heat to a gentle simmer and cook for 5 minutes.

Remove from the heat and cool a little.

Remove the bay leaves, and purée using a blender.

MUSHROOM PRAWN STUFFING

4 Tbsp (60 mL) olive oil, divided

5 cups (1.25 L) roughly chopped button mushrooms (12 oz/340 g)

1 large shallot, minced

1 clove garlic, minced

11 oz (310 g) raw prawns, peeled and finely chopped

2 Tbsp (30 mL) chopped chives

Juice of 1 lemon

Sea salt and freshly ground black pepper

Heat 2 Tbsp (30 mL) of the olive oil in a medium frying pan, add the mushrooms and cook until all the liquid is cooked off and the mushrooms are dry and browned.

Add the shallot and garlic and cook for another 2 minutes.

Add the prawns and the remaining 2 Tbsp (30 mL) olive oil, and cook for a further 5 minutes.

Add the chives and lemon juice, and season with salt and pepper. Set aside to cool.

If you're at a farmers' market in Vancouver, look out for Glorious Organics (at the Organic Farm Connection booth), who've been part of the restaurant program since I came to CinCin over four years ago. In summertime, they provide salad greens, fruits and vegetables, and herbs. Their products are unique with exceptional flavour and cannot be sourced anywhere else.

Glorious Organics green leaf salad — edible blossoms and pickled ramps — elderflower dressing

SERVES 4

Elderflower Vinegar
(for the Elderflower Dressing) *overleaf*

Elderflower Syrup
(for the Elderflower Dressing) *overleaf*

16 Pickled Ramps *below*

½ cup (125 mL) Elderflower Dressing *overleaf*

½ lb (220 g) mixed organic salad and herb leaves

Maldon salt

16 mixed edible plant and herb flowers, including elderflowers, to garnish

At least a day before serving, start the elderflower vinegar and syrup.

You can also prepare the pickled ramps beforehand, as their flavour improves over time.

On the day of serving, prepare the elderflower dressing.

To prepare the salad, cut the ramps into bite-sized pieces, and in a nonreactive mixing bowl, combine the salad and herb leaves with the ramps, salt and dressing. Using your hands, gently dress the leaves.

Divide the salad to 4 plates, arranging an attractive pile on each plate. Sprinkle with the edible flowers.

PICKLED RAMPS

1 recipe Pickling Liquid *page 213*

16 ramps (wild leeks) or green onions

Prepare the pickling liquid.

Peel the outer leaves from the ramps and clean off any dirt. If using green onions, remove the outer skin and clean until white.

Place in a pot, barely cover with the strained pickling liquid and bring to a boil. In the meantime, set a large bowl over ice. Remove the pot from the heat, and transfer the ramps and liquid to the bowl to cool.

You can use this immediately, but note that the flavour improves over time; the ramps can be stored in the pickling liquid for up to 6 months in the fridge.

Continued overleaf

WINE NOTE At the restaurant we pair this dish with a local Sauvignon Blanc, such as Pentâge Barrel Fermented 2013 from BC. In a pinch, Marlborough Sauvignon Blanc would also work.

We also buy our fresh elderflowers at the farmers' market.
The recipes for elderflower syrup and elderflower vinegar
make more than you'll need for the dressing. Bar manager
David Wolowidnyk puts the syrup in his cocktails. You can
also add it to a homemade sorbetto or granita. The vinegar
can be used in any salad vinaigrette.

ELDERFLOWER VINEGAR

1 cup (250 mL) **fresh elderflowers**

1 cup (250 mL) **champagne vinegar**

Cut off the elderflower stems, and place the flowers in a clean jar. Pour the vinegar over the flowers and let it infuse overnight, either at room temperature or in the fridge.

The following day, strain the mixture and discard the elderflowers. The vinegar keeps for at least 3 months.

ELDERFLOWER SYRUP

1 cup (250 mL) **water**

½ lb (220 g) **granulated sugar** (1¼ cups/310 mL)

2 cups (500 mL) **fresh elderflowers**

Heat the water in a heavy-bottomed pot. Add the sugar and dissolve. Remove from the heat and add the elderflowers.

Let it cool, then place the pot in the fridge and let it infuse overnight.

The following day, strain the mixture and discard the elderflowers.

ELDERFLOWER DRESSING (Makes about 1 cup)

1 shallot

2 tsp (10 mL) **Dijon mustard**

1 egg yolk

1 Tbsp (15 mL) **Elderflower Vinegar**

⅔ cup (160 mL) **canola or sunflower oil**

1 Tbsp (15 mL) **Elderflower Syrup**

Sea salt

Combine the shallots, mustard, egg yolk and vinegar in a food processor or blender and blend. With the machine running, slowly pour in the oil, and continue blending until thick and creamy. Season with Elderflower Syrup and salt to taste, thinning with water if necessary. Aim for the consistency of heavy cream.

Gnocchi Romani — fontina, prosciutto di Parma and pickled daikon

SERVES 4

16 ribbons of **Pickled Daikon** *below*

4 pieces (½ recipe) **Gnocchi Romani** *page 164*

4 tsp (20 mL) **unsalted butter**

4 oz (110 g) **grated fontina** (1 cup/250 mL)

12 slices prosciutto di Parma

Good-quality olive oil, for finishing

Prepare the pickled daikon.

Prepare the gnocchi romani; follow the steps until you put the shaped gnocchi in the fridge to set.

Preheat the oven to 400°F (200°C).

Line a 9 × 13-inch (23 × 33 cm) baking sheet with parchment, and lightly grease the parchment with oil.

Place each piece of gnocchi on the baking sheet. Dot the butter over the pieces, and sprinkle with fontina.

Bake for 10 minutes, or until the cheese is melted, bubbling and turning golden brown.

Remove from the oven, and place a gnocchi on each serving plate.

Neatly place 3 slices of prosciutto next to the gnocchi.

Remove 16 ribbons of daikon from the pickling liquid and shake dry. Drape 4 ribbons over each gnocchi. Drizzle with olive oil and serve.

PICKLED DAIKON

1 recipe Pickling Liquid *page 213*

1 large daikon radish

You'll be pickling more daikon than you need for this recipe. Cut the ribbons into smaller pieces, and it's a nice refreshing addition to salads.

Prepare the pickling liquid.

Peel the daikon, and cut it into thin ribbons with a mandolin.

Place the daikon in a pot and barely cover with the pickling liquid. (You might use less than the 5 cups/1.25 L.)

Bring to a boil. In the meantime, set a large bowl over ice. Remove the pot from the heat, and transfer the daikon and liquid to the bowl to cool.

You can use this immediately, but note that the flavour improves over time; the daikon can be stored in the pickling liquid for up to 3 weeks in the fridge.

WINE NOTE This is a rich dish, and you need a wine with some body and weight. At CinCin we serve Quintodecimo Exultet Fiano di Avellino 2012 from Campania. At home, any Fiano would be a success.

SALT

Salt is not a mere taste enhancer. It is an essential component in the human body's chemistry. We require it to live, which probably explains why we crave it, and perhaps overindulge at times. Salt has a whole rainbow of flavours and accents, some heading into what passes for sweetness, others clearly about salinity only.

You can choose from dozens of sea salts without even considering the many artisanal, flavoured salts available. Add kosher and regular iodized salts, and you have quite a range of options for seasoning your food.

Whether pink from the Himalaya or cloudy grey from the shores of Brittany, coarse-grained salt is used to garnish almost anything, but most particularly any sort of salad. Kosher salt, a rather mild salt, builds layers of flavour to create a more rounded palate at the end. Beyond garnish and seasoning, CinCin uses Himalayan pink salt in the brine for its pork belly.

In addition to being a great culinary advantage in itself, salt helps open the palate to other, related flavours, and even provides lift to aromas.

CORNERSTONE
INGREDIENT

Grilled romaine lettuce and smoked salmon — pickled red onion, crunchy chickpeas, rosemary and chili

¾ cup (185 mL) **Rosemary, Chili and Anchovy Dressing** *below*

Crunchy Chickpeas *overleaf*

12 rings **Pickled Red Onion** *overleaf*

2 heads romaine lettuce, cut in half lengthwise

6 Tbsp (90 mL) extra virgin olive oil

Sea salt and freshly ground black pepper

12 slices of smoked sockeye salmon

Garlic chips (from the dressing), for garnish

Chopped Italian (flat-leaf) parsley, for garnish

Prepare the dressing, chickpeas and pickled onion, and set aside.

Light a wood-fired barbecue, or preheat a gas or charcoal grill or cast-iron grill pan.

Dress each romaine half with about 1 ½ Tbsp (22 mL) of olive oil. Spread the leaves with your fingers, and season liberally with salt and pepper.

Place romaine halves on the hot grill, cut side down. Cook until well coloured. Turn and repeat. When both sides are charred, transfer to the 4 serving plates, cut side up.

Spoon 3 Tbsp (45 mL) of the dressing over each lettuce. Drape 3 slices of the smoked salmon over each lettuce. Add 3 rings of the pickled onion and a sprinkle of chickpeas, garlic and parsley, and serve warm.

ROSEMARY, CHILI AND ANCHOVY DRESSING

12 anchovy fillets, packed in oil

¾ cup (185 mL) extra virgin olive oil

8 cloves garlic, thinly sliced

4 pinches dried chili flakes

1 sprig fresh rosemary, leaves only, roughly chopped

Drain the anchovies and pat dry.

Pour the olive oil into a small heavy-bottomed pot, add the garlic and cook over medium heat until the garlic turns golden brown. Strain the oil into a small bowl or measuring cup, reserving the garlic for the finished plate.

Return the oil to the pot. Add the chili, rosemary and anchovies while the oil is still warm and set aside for about 30 minutes. The chili and rosemary will infuse the oil, and the anchovies will disintegrate, forming a warm and fragrant dressing. *Continued overleaf*

WINE NOTE A rosé is called for. If you're in the mood for bubbles, try Taittinger Prestige rosé n/v. If you prefer a still, I suggest Costaripa RosaMara rosé 2014 from Italy.

CRUNCHY CHICKPEAS

¾ cup (185 mL) **canned or cooked chickpeas**

Canola oil, for deep-frying

Sea salt, to taste

Preheat the oil in a deep fryer to 320°F (160°C).

Drain and rinse the chickpeas and pat dry.

Have ready a large plate or tray lined with paper towels. Fry the chickpeas in the hot oil until crispy. Drain on the paper towels, and season with salt.

PICKLED RED ONION

1 large red onion, peeled

6 Tbsp (90 mL) **olive oil, for dressing the onion**

Sea salt and freshly ground black pepper

4 sprigs fresh thyme

2 cups (500 mL) **red wine vinegar**

You'll have pickled onions left over after making the grilled romaine recipe. They're great on burgers.

Peel the onion and cut off the root end. Light the wood-fired barbecue you'll also be using for the romaine, or preheat a gas or charcoal grill or cast-iron grill pan.

Cut the onion crosswise into ¼-inch (6 mm) slices. Dress each slice with olive oil, and season with salt and pepper.

Grill the slices until they are nicely charred, about 4 minutes each side.

Transfer the slices to a large sealed container, cover the onion with the red wine vinegar and add the thyme. Marinate in the fridge for at least 24 hours.

Wood-roasted and smoked tomato soup

SERVES 6

4 lbs (1.8 kg) **ripe red tomatoes (any variety)**

Olive oil, for dressing the tomatoes

1 cup (250 mL) **olive oil, for sautéing the vegetables**

6 large cloves **garlic, crushed with back of knife**

1 stalk **lemon grass, crushed with back of knife**

4 fresh or dried **bay leaves**

4 sprigs **fresh thyme**

4 sprigs **fresh rosemary**

4 medium **onions, thinly sliced**

4 stalks **celery, thinly sliced**

1 bulb **fennel, thinly sliced**

½ **fresh red chili, seeded and thinly sliced**

2 tsp (10 mL) **tomato purée**

2 tsp (10 mL) **granulated sugar**

Juice of 1 lemon

Sea salt and freshly ground black pepper, to taste

Good-quality olive oil, for finishing

A wood-fired oven or barbecue will give you the finest results. You can also use your oven, preheated to 400°F (200°C).

Cut the tomatoes in half, and place on an 11 × 17-inch (28 × 43 cm) baking sheet, cut side up. Drizzle with a little olive oil, and roast in the oven box until they take on colour and start to collapse. This will take 20 minutes in a box, and 40 minutes in a regular oven. Remove from the oven and set aside.

Heat the olive oil in a large frying pan with the garlic, lemon grass, bay leaves, thyme and rosemary. When the oil is hot, add the onions, celery, fennel and chili. Cook until the vegetables start to soften.

Spread in a single even layer across 1 or 2 baking sheets. Roast in the oven box, stirring frequently, until the vegetables are soft and nicely coloured. Again, this will take 20 minutes in a box, and 40 minutes in a regular oven. Remove from the oven and set aside.

When cool enough to handle, remove the bay leaves, thyme, rosemary and lemon grass.

In a large bowl, thoroughly combine the onion mixture with the roasted tomatoes, tomato paste, sugar and lemon juice. Purée the mixture in small batches in a blender, and then push through a coarse sieve into a large pot.

Add enough cold water to bring the soup to a pouring consistency (the consistency of heavy cream). Reheat and season with salt and pepper.

Pour into 6 soup bowls, and drizzle with olive oil.

WINE NOTE **A local rosé, such as Liquidity or Sage Hills, would be fantastic.**

The goal here is to release the flavour of the vegetables through slow and gentle cooking. We do the same thing with soffritto (page 213), which is used in many of our recipes.

La minestra — vegetable soup

SERVES 6

3 Tbsp (45 mL) **extra virgin olive oil**

1 end piece prosciutto di Parma (about ½ lb/220 g) **or 4 slices bacon, cut in half**

2 onions, minced

4 carrots, cut into ½-inch (1 cm) **dice**

2 leeks, white part only, cut into ½-inch (1 cm) **dice**

6 stalks celery, cut into ½-inch (1 cm) **dice**

1 bunch Tuscan kale (also called Lacinato or dinosaur kale; you can substitute other kinds), cut into ¼-inch (6 mm) **strips**

2 sprigs fresh thyme

1 sprig fresh rosemary

1 cup (250 mL) **tomato passata** (7 oz/200 g)

8 cups (2 L) **White Chicken Stock** *page 215*

1 cup (250 mL) **cooked borlotti (cranberry or Romano) beans**

1 ¼ cups (310 mL) **cooked cornetti pasta**

Good-quality olive oil, for finishing

6 Tbsp (90 mL) **chopped Italian (flat-leaf) parsley, for garnish**

Freshly grated Parmesan, for garnish

In a heavy-bottomed pot, heat the olive oil and add the prosciutto or bacon. Cook over low heat until the juices run, being careful not to brown, about 10 minutes.

Add the onions, carrots, leeks and celery, cover and continue cooking very gently for a further 10 minutes. Do not allow the vegetables to colour.

Add the kale, thyme, rosemary and tomato passata. Cover and cook until the kale is wilted and tender, about 10 minutes.

When the vegetables are tender, with very little resistance when you bite into them, add the stock just enough to cover. Bring to a boil, lower the heat to a gentle simmer and cook until the vegetables are completely tender.

Add the cooked beans and pasta, bring to a boil again, then turn the heat off. Season with salt and pepper.

Divide between 6 soup bowls. Drizzle with olive oil, sprinkle with chopped parsley and grate Parmesan over each bowl before serving.

WINE NOTE An Italian white such as Vermentino or Pinot Grigio would be ideal. At CinCin we pair this with La Spinetta Vermentino 2013 from Tuscany.

Corn soup infused with basil

SERVES 8

8 cobs corn, husks attached

4 oz (110 g) **unsalted butter** (½ cup/120 mL), divided

2 cups (500 mL) **minced onion** (14 oz/400 g), divided

8 cups (2 L) **water**

½ cup (125 mL) **heavy cream**

1 small bunch fresh basil

Sea salt and freshly ground black pepper

Husks prevent the corn kernels from drying out, so always try to buy corn with them on. Shuck the corn, cut the kernels from the corn cobs and cut the cobs in half. Set aside the corn kernels and cobs.

Melt ¼ cup (60 mL) of the butter in a heavy-bottomed pot. Add 1 cup (250 mL) of the diced onion, cover and sweat for 10 minutes, being careful not to brown.

Add the halved corn cobs and a pinch of salt, and cook for a further 5 minutes.

Add the water, bring to a boil, reduce the heat and simmer for 30 minutes.

Remove the pot from the heat, and let it infuse for a further 30 minutes. Strain the stock and set aside.

In a clean pot, melt the remaining ¼ cup (60 mL) butter, and add the remaining 1 cup (250 mL) onion. Cover and sweat for 10 minutes, without browning.

Add the corn kernels and a good pinch of salt, and sweat for a further 5 minutes.

Add the corn stock, bring to a simmer and cook for 30 minutes.

Add the cream, and gently simmer for a further 5 minutes.

Remove the pot from the heat. Using a blender, purée the soup until smooth, and then push the purée through a fine-meshed sieve into a pot. Add the whole stems and leaves of basil, and let it infuse for 30 minutes.

Remove the basil, season with salt and pepper and gently reheat before serving.

WINE NOTE At CinCin we pair this dish with a Tuscan Chardonnay such as Castello di Monsanto Chardonnay 2012. A local option is Blue Mountain Reserve Chardonnay.

BASIL

You will not find us using anything out of season. As much as I love each ingredient, we have to accept that most things are seasonal, and embrace that as a good kind of challenge—to use the foods that are relevant and available, in their own cycle.

Fresh and seasonal is a CinCin mantra. But with herbs, it is really a necessity. While certain herbs can do well in dried form (oregano comes to mind), fresh herbs rule, and the spotlight often shines on basil.

Multicultural and multifaceted, basil can be grown indoors year-round. The Italian version, known as sweet basil, has over a hundred different cultivars, making for interesting variety in relative sweetness and pungency. Thai basil is spicier, and can even boast a bit of anise flavour. Each type is appropriate to certain cuisines and dishes. Exotics such as lemon basil, purple basil, Siam Queen basil and holy basil also have their own distinct flavour characteristics.

Unlike most other herbs, basil is best used uncooked, as a finishing flourish or part of a salad. At CinCin, even the basil stems are used, to lend an ingeniously delicious lift to a corn-cob-based vegetable stock. ————————

CORNERSTONE
INGREDIENT

Mushroom soup — thyme croutons and olive oil

Olive oil, for the croutons

3 slices white bread or stale baguette,
cut into ½-inch (1 cm) dice

1 large sprig fresh thyme

2 cloves garlic, crushed with back of knife

1 Tbsp (15 mL) unsalted butter

½ onion, minced

½ leek, white part only, roughly chopped

18 oz (500 g) button mushrooms (8 cups/2 L),
thinly sliced

1 small potato, peeled and diced

3 cups (750 mL) White Chicken Stock *page 215*

3 cups (750 mL) heavy cream

Sea salt and freshly ground white pepper

Good-quality olive oil, for finishing

Preheat the oven to 375°F (190°C).

Heat an 11 × 17-inch (28 × 43 cm) baking sheet in
the oven. When hot, drizzle the baking sheet with
a small amount of olive oil. Add the diced bread,
thyme and garlic. Toast, turning occasionally, until
golden brown. Remove and discard the garlic and
thyme and set croutons aside.

Melt the butter in a large, heavy-bottomed pot.
Add the onion, leek and mushrooms. Cover and
sweat over low heat for 20 minutes.

Meanwhile, in a medium pot combine the potato,
stock and cream, bring to a boil and simmer until
the potato is cooked, about 10 minutes.

Add the potato mixture to the mushroom mixture,
and simmer for 10 minutes.

Using a blender or food processor, purée the soup,
then strain through a fine-meshed sieve.

Reheat and correct the seasoning with salt and
white pepper.

Divide into 6 bowls, topping each with 6 to 8
croutons and a drizzle of olive oil.

WINE NOTE For me, it's a simple mathematical formula:
mushrooms = Pinot Noir. Try one of our local offerings
like Spierhead or Foxtrot from the Okanagan valley.

Vancouver Island octopus and Ibérico chorizo — new season potatoes, fennel, orange and celery leaves

SERVES 4

½ cup (125 mL) **Orange Oil** *page 223*

⅔ cup (160 mL) **Classic Vinaigrette** *page 222*

1 large **double-suckered octopus**
(7 lbs 1 oz/3.5 kg)

2 cups (500 mL) **olive oil**, for dressing and cooking octopus

Sea salt

6 medium **new-season potatoes** (preferably Sieglinde/German butter or fingerling)

1 bulb **fennel**, with fronds

4 oz (110 g) **Ibérico chorizo**, thinly sliced

Freshly ground black pepper

1 cup (250 mL) **celery leaves**, lightly packed

Pinch of chopped Italian (flat-leaf) parsley

PREPARING OCTOPUS

Clean the tentacles by placing them in a stainless steel bowl and drizzling with olive oil and a generous amount of salt. Massage for 2 minutes. Let stand for 15 minutes, then rinse under cold running water and pat dry.

Cut the head off just below the beak. Separate the tentacles by cutting between each of them. Place in a heavy-bottomed pot with 2 Tbsp (30 mL) water. Cover and place on low heat. The octopus will begin to release liquid as it warms. Within about 45 minutes, it will be covered and start cooking in its own juices. The octopus is done when you can easily pierce the tentacles with the tip of a knife or squash them between your fingers. Then cut the tentacles into 3-inch (8 cm) pieces.

Begin preparing the orange oil 3 days ahead.

Prepare the classic vinaigrette.

Prepare the octopus (see tip).

Put the whole unpeeled potatoes in a medium pot with just enough water to cover and a generous pinch of salt. Bring to a boil, lower the heat to a gentle simmer and cook until tender. Allow to cool in the water.

When cool enough to handle, remove the skin with a sharp knife, and slice into ¼-inch (6 mm) discs. While still warm, dress the potatoes liberally with the vinaigrette (reserving enough vinaigrette for the fennel and celery leaves).

Have ready a bowl or tray of ice. Trim the base and the core from the fennel, and remove the stalks and the tough outer layer. Using a mandolin or knife, slice the fennel crosswise into thin slices. Immediately place on the ice. After 10 minutes, remove the fennel and dry in a salad spinner. It should be crisp.

Light a wood-fired barbecue, or preheat a gas or charcoal grill or cast-iron grill pan.

Use 8-inch (20 cm) plates to serve. Lay the chorizo in a circle on each of the 4 plates. Lay 6 slices of the dressed potato on top of the chorizo.

Coat the octopus lightly in olive oil, season with salt and pepper and grill until you see grill marks. Diagonally slice the octopus into ¾-inch-thick (2 cm) pieces. Place 6 pieces of octopus on top of the potatoes. Dress with a little of the orange oil.

Chop the fennel fronds and celery leaves. Toss in a salad bowl with the sliced fennel and a pinch of parsley. Dress with a little vinaigrette and season with a pinch of salt. Mix thoroughly, then place a handful on top of the octopus and in the centre of each plate. Drizzle over a little more orange oil, and serve. *Continued overleaf*

WINE NOTE **This dish calls for something citrusy and savoury, and that wine is Vermentino. Try one from Sardinia. Capichera Vermentino di Gallura 2014 is one of the best.**

Goat cheese salad – golden and Chioggia beets, smoked orange vinaigrette and pistachios

2 Tbsp (30 mL) **Smoked Orange Vinaigrette** *facing page*

8 cups (2 L) **water**

¾ cup (185 mL) **champagne or white wine vinegar**

7 Tbsp (105 mL) **granulated sugar**

2 Tbsp (30 mL) **salt**

2 ¼ lbs (1 kg) **medium-sized golden beets**

2 ¼ lbs (1 kg) **medium-sized Chioggia (candy cane) beets**

Goat Cheese Cream *facing page*

2 Tbsp (30 mL) **Classic Vinaigrette** *page 222*

1 handful salad leaves (frisée, radicchio, arugula)

Extra virgin olive oil

2–2 ½ oz (60–70 g) **shelled pistachios** (¹/₃ cup/80 mL)**, dry-roasted and broken**

Sea salt and freshly ground black pepper

2–4 Cherriette (or any red-skinned) radishes

Prepare the smoked orange vinaigrette.

In a large pot, combine the water, vinegar, sugar and salt. Add the beets and adjust the liquid to cover them completely (if necessary, increase the recipe).

Cover the liquid with a cartouche (see the tip on page 95) to keep the beets below the surface. Bring to a boil, lower the heat to a simmer and cook gently. When the beets can be easily pierced with a knife and are floating, remove the pot from the heat and allow to cool in the pot.

Meanwhile, prepare the goat cheese cream and the classic vinaigrette.

Peel the beets, and cut into discs ⅛ inch (3 mm) thick using either a mandolin or a sharp knife. Set aside.

Rinse the salad leaves in cold water and spin dry.

For each plate, arrange the beet slices in a circle ½ inch (1 cm) from the edge, slightly overlapping and alternating the golden and Chioggia. Dress with the orange vinaigrette (about 2 Tbsp/30 mL per plate) and drizzle with a little olive oil.

Place a spoonful (about 2 Tbsp/30 mL) of the goat cheese cream in the centre of each plate. Sprinkle with pistachios and season with salt and pepper.

Dress the salad leaves with the classic vinaigrette, and neatly place them around the goat cheese and over the beets.

Using a mandolin, shave 6 slices of radish over each plate, and serve.

About 6 oranges

2 Tbsp (30 mL) **sherry vinegar**

2 Tbsp (30 mL) **extra virgin olive oil**

Sea salt and freshly ground black pepper

Granulated sugar, to taste

First roast the oranges. Place the oranges in smouldering coals or the smouldering embers of a wood fire, and leave them until the oranges become completely black and charred. You can also just grill the whole oranges, or use tongs to hold the oranges over a gas flame. Let the oranges cool completely.

Juice the oranges. You should have 1 ½ cups (375 mL). Place the orange juice in a pot, and bring to a boil over medium heat. Lower the heat and simmer until the juice is reduced to ⅓ cup (80 mL). Allow to cool.

Stir in the vinegar and olive oil. Season to taste with salt and pepper. Add just enough sugar to balance the acidity.

GOAT CHEESE CREAM

4 oz (110 g) **goat cheese** (½ cup/125 mL)

¼ cup (60 mL) **heavy cream**

Sea salt and freshly ground black pepper, to taste

Place the goat cheese in the bowl of an electric mixer. Using the whisk attachment, work until the cheese becomes soft and light.

With the mixer running at high speed, add the cream in a slow, steady stream until incorporated. Season with salt and pepper.

WINE NOTE This is a tricky wine pairing, but one wine comes to mind that can match the different components in this dish: Andre Felici Il Cantico della Figura, Verdicchio del Castelli di Jesi 2012. A long name and even longer finish! Any reputable wine shop will have a quality Verdicchio available if you cannot find Andre Felici.

Salad of two endives — Gorgonzola, walnuts and pear — walnut vinaigrette

½ cup (125 mL) **Walnut Vinaigrette** *below*

4 heads red Belgian endive

4 heads green Belgian endive

4 oz (110 g) **Gorgonzola cheese**

3 oz (85 g) **toasted walnuts** (²/₃ cup/160 mL)

2 ripe pears, unpeeled

Sea salt and freshly ground black pepper

¼ cup (60 mL) **chopped Italian (flat-leaf) parsley, for garnish**

Prepare the walnut vinaigrette.

Trim the stem from the endive, and cut ½ inch (1 cm) from the base. Cut the endive in half lengthwise. Trim away the white core. Rinse the leaves in cold water, and either spin-dry or pat dry with a tea towel or paper towels. Set aside in a salad bowl large enough to hold all the leaves.

Break the Gorgonzola and walnuts into small pieces.

Cut the pears in half, remove the cores and slice the halves into thin pieces about ⅛ inch (3 mm) thick.

Drizzle most of the vinaigrette over the endive leaves, reserving 1 to 2 Tbsp (15–30 mL) for finishing the plates. Season with salt and pepper, and mix gently with a fork or spoon, being careful not to bruise the leaves.

Arrange the dressed leaves on 4 plates. Evenly distribute the pear, Gorgonzola and walnuts over the endive leaves. Drizzle the remaining vinaigrette over the 4 plates, and then sprinkle with parsley.

WALNUT VINAIGRETTE

1 Tbsp (15 mL) **Dijon mustard**

1 ½ Tbsp (22 mL) **white wine vinegar**

1 ½ Tbsp (22 mL) **fresh lemon juice**

½ cup (125 mL) **walnut oil**

Sea salt and freshly ground black pepper

Whisk together the mustard, vinegar and lemon juice. Keep whisking as you slowly pour in the walnut oil. Season with salt and pepper.

WINE NOTE A Pecorino would be fun—the wine, not the cheese! Pasetti Pecorino 2012 from Abruzzo would do nicely.

Tuna tartare — lemon, olive oil and crostini

2 Tbsp (30 mL) **Lemon Oil** *page 223*

1 lb (450 g) **sushi-grade albacore tuna**

Zest of 1 lemon

Maldon salt

¼ cup (60 mL) **finely chopped chives**

1 **store-bought baguette**

Extra virgin olive oil, for the baguette slices and for finishing

Fine sea salt

Maldon salt

Chopped Italian (flat-leaf) parsley, for garnish

Microgreens (beet, chard, brassicas, arugula, herbs), for garnish

Prepare the lemon oil at least 3 days before you plan to use it.

Prepare an ice bath for the tuna by fitting one bowl inside another bowl filled with ice.

Clean the tuna of any sinew, and cut into ⅓-inch (8 mm) dice. Place immediately into the bowl that's on top of the ice.

Season the tuna with the lemon zest, Maldon salt, lemon oil and chives.

For the crostini, preheat the oven to 425°F (225°C). Slice the baguette into very thin rounds, about ⅛ inch (3 mm) thick. Place on a baking sheet and drizzle with olive oil. Bake until golden brown, then season with fine sea salt.

Spoon the tuna onto 4 plates. Drizzle over a little more lemon oil and olive oil.

Sprinkle with a pinch of Maldon salt and parsley, and finish with a small handful of microgreens.

Place the crostini on the side of each plate and serve.

WINE NOTE **If you want to venture off the beaten path, try Arnaldo Caprai Grechetto 2012 from Umbria. Locally, Daydreamer Pinot Gris 2013 will make you happy.**

Wild prawns wood-grilled on a rosemary branch — hummus, chili and buckwheat — watercress

½ cup (125 mL) **Chickpea Purée** *page 154*

2 Tbsp (30 mL) **Classic Vinaigrette** *page 222*

16–20 large wild prawns, heads and shells removed

4 sprigs fresh rosemary, about 8 inches (20 cm) long with the leaves intact

Extra virgin olive oil

Sea salt and freshly ground black pepper

4 tsp (20 mL) buckwheat, toasted

6 Tbsp (90 mL) **Chili Oil** *page 222*

4 small handfuls watercress

Prepare the chickpea purée (hummus).

Prepare the vinaigrette.

Light a wood-fired barbecue, or preheat a gas or charcoal grill or cast-iron grill pan.

Skewer 4 to 5 prawns onto each rosemary branch through the centre of the body. Dress with a drizzle of olive oil, and season with salt and a grind of black pepper. Grill the prawns, turning 4 times until evenly cooked (they'll turn red and have grill marks).

Divide the hummus between 4 plates, and top with the toasted buckwheat. Place a skewer of prawns on top, and drizzle over with chili oil.

Dress the watercress with classic vinaigrette, arrange on one side of the plate and serve.

Fried zucchini blossoms — Montasio, goat cheese and Parmesan — arugula and red radish

Three-Cheese Stuffing *overleaf*

Canola oil, for deep-frying

1 ¾ cups (435 mL) **tempura flour** (7 oz/200 g)

8 **zucchini blossoms** (male or female)

4 handfuls **arugula**

Classic Vinaigrette *page 222*

4 **Cherriette** (or any red-skinned) **radishes**

Good-quality olive oil, for finishing

Sea salt and freshly ground black pepper

Prepare the three-cheese stuffing and set aside.

Preheat canola oil in a deep fryer to 360°F (182°C).

Prepare a tempura batter following the manufacturer's guidelines for the ratio of ice water to flour.

Dust and clean the zucchini blossoms of any soil.

Place the cheese stuffing in a piping bag, and pipe into the heart of each blossom. Use enough of the cheese mixture to fit into the base of the flower bud without spilling out through the leaves. Fold the petals around the mixture.

Dredge the blossoms in the tempura batter, and shake off any excess.

Have ready a large plate or tray lined with paper towels. Without overcrowding the fryer, drop the blossoms into the hot oil, and cook until they float and just start to turn brown. Drain on the paper towels, and keep warm while the remaining blossoms are cooked.

Dress the arugula with the vinaigrette. Using a mandolin or sharp knife, thinly slice the radishes.

Divide the arugula between 4 plates, place 2 zucchini blossoms on each plate and sprinkle the radish slices over the top. Drizzle with olive oil, and season with salt and pepper. *Continued overleaf*

WINE NOTE **Try this dish with a California Chardonnay or Viognier.**

1 medium Yukon gold potato

Salt (preferably rock salt or kosher salt), for baking the potato

4 oz (110 g) firm goat cheese (½ cup/125 mL)

2 oz (60 g) grated Montasio or cheddar cheese (½ cup/125 mL)

1 ¾ oz (50 g) grated Parmesan (½ cup/125 mL)

1 egg

2 Tbsp (30 mL) chopped chives

2 Tbsp (30 mL) chopped Italian (flat-leaf) parsley

Sea salt and freshly ground black pepper

Preheat the oven to 400°F (200°C).

Fill a small ovenproof frying pan or baking sheet with salt to a depth of a ½ inch (1 cm). Prick the potato all around using a sharp knife, and lay it on the bed of salt. Bake until it's completely tender, about 1 hour. (The salt seasons the potato as well as keeps it dry while it bakes.)

While still warm, cut in half and scoop out the flesh. (Reserve the skin for another use, or compost.) Pass the flesh through a food mill or potato ricer, or push it through a coarse sieve, and set aside to cool.

When cool, add the cheeses, egg, herbs and salt and pepper, and beat together until fully combined.

PARMESAN

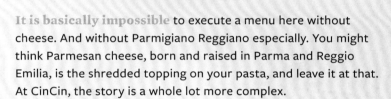

It is basically impossible to execute a menu here without cheese. And without Parmigiano Reggiano especially. You might think Parmesan cheese, born and raised in Parma and Reggio Emilia, is the shredded topping on your pasta, and leave it at that. At CinCin, the story is a whole lot more complex.

For one thing, Parmesan for the final dish is not prepped before the dish is ready. A chunk is inserted into a small hand grinder, and your topping comes fresh from the grinder onto your pasta or risotto. CinCin works with Italian goods supplier Cioffi's to bring the cheese to the restaurant in one-kilo wedges, from which cooks and servers alike take what they need.

Parmesan can accompany to great effect a beef carpaccio or a plate of zucchini blossoms with arugula, radishes and perhaps another cheese or two. It is also a key ingredient in the house-made *pistous*.

Grana Padano, a great Italian hard cheese in its own right, is often used in dishes where its slightly milder, creamier flavour is preferred. For example, it is used in place of Parmesan to fold into the risottos as they are finishing on the stove.

Parmesan can benefit with age, the flavours growing more earthy and rich, so you can buy it in various vintages. The older ones make a fabulous centrepiece on a dessert plate or cheese platter, and can be paired to great effect with aged balsamic vinegar. ———————

CORNERSTONE
INGREDIENT

Buffalo mozzarella with Meyer lemon — three endives — Parmesan and olive oil

½ cup (125 mL) **Meyer Lemon Vinaigrette** *page 222*

¼ cup (60 mL) **Classic Vinaigrette** *page 222*

4 heads green Belgian endive

4 heads red Belgian endive

1 head frisée (curly endive)

2 Tbsp (30 mL) chopped Italian (flat-leaf) parsley

Two ½ lb (220 g) portions buffalo mozzarella

Good-quality olive oil, for finishing

Sea salt and freshly ground black pepper

Freshly grated Parmesan, for finishing

Prepare the 2 vinaigrettes.

Trim the stem from the green and red Belgian endive, and cut ½ inch (1 cm) from the base. Cut the endive in half lengthwise. Trim away the white core. Rinse the leaves in cold water, and either spin-dry or pat dry with a tea towel or paper towels. Place in a mixing bowl. Separate the leaves of the frisée, and rinse and spin-dry/pat dry. Add to the mixing bowl, along with the chopped parsley.

Cut or tear each ball of mozzarella into 2 pieces.

Spread 2 Tbsp (30 mL) of the Meyer lemon vinaigrette over the base of 4 plates. Place the mozzarella on top of the vinaigrette just off the centre.

Drizzle the classic vinaigrette over the endive and frisée, and toss gently, making sure all the leaves are lightly coated.

Build a salad of the leaves on each plate next to the mozzarella. Dress the mozzarella with a generous amount of olive oil, and season with salt and pepper. Grate about 1 ½ Tbsp (22 mL) of Parmesan over each salad, and serve.

WINE NOTE Try this with a wine from the south of Italy, like a Fiano from Campania or a Vermentino from Sardinia.

Chicken liver pâté with prosciutto di Parma and pickled romanesco — grilled Red Fife sourdough

Pickled Romanesco, 8 florets per serving
facing page

2 eggs

½ lb (220 g) **chicken livers, cleaned**

½ lb (220 g) **unsalted butter** (½ cup/125 mL)

3 Tbsp (45 mL) **port wine**

3 Tbsp (45 mL) **brandy**

¼ cup (60 mL) **thinly sliced shallots**
(2 oz/60 g)

1 clove garlic, thinly sliced

½ sprig fresh thyme

½ tsp (2.5 mL) **Himalayan pink salt**

Freshly ground black pepper

12 slices prosciutto di Parma

8 slices Red Fife sourdough
(or ciabatta) bread

Extra virgin olive oil and sea salt,
for the bread

Prepare the pickled romanesco up to a month ahead.

Crack the eggs in a medium bowl and add the livers, and bring to room temperature (about 1 ½ hours).

Melt the butter, then let it cool but don't let it solidify.

In a small saucepan, combine the port, brandy, shallots, garlic and thyme. Bring to a boil and reduce until three-quarters of the original volume (takes no longer than 1 minute). Discard the sprig of thyme.

Put the liver, eggs and shallot-garlic mixture into a blender, and blend for 5 seconds. With the blender running at moderate speed, pour in the butter a little at a time until it is all incorporated and the mixture is smooth and creamy.

Pass through a fine-meshed sieve. Add the salt and pepper.

Preheat the oven to 250°F (120°C).

Heat a kettle of water. Pour the mixture into four 3-inch (8 cm) ramekins, and place in a 9 × 13-inch (23 × 33 cm) baking pan. Pour enough hot water into the baking pan to come halfway up the ramekins. Bake for 45 minutes. The liver should be barely cooked and should jiggle when shaken. Remove the ramekins from the tray, and cool completely.

Preheat a gas or charcoal grill or cast-iron grill pan (or use a wood-fired barbecue if you have one going).

Place 3 slices of prosciutto on one side of each plate. On the other side place the ramekin. Remove the romanesco from the liquid and pat dry. Sprinkle about 8 florets over the prosciutto.

Dress the bread slices with a little olive oil and grill. Season with a little salt, place on the side of each plate and serve.

The pâté is a cornerstone recipe at CinCin. Romanesco is one of the most visually striking of vegetables with its geometric shapes—and it has a delicious nutty flavour too. Pickle it, and its acidic, sweet, and sour flavour will be a nice contrast with the rich pâté. (Cauliflower is an acceptable substitute if you can't find romanesco.)

PICKLED ROMANESCO

1 recipe Pickling Liquid *page 213*

1 head romanesco, broken into florets

Prepare the pickling liquid.

Place the strained pickling liquid in a large pot, add the romanesco florets and bring to a boil. Remove from the heat and allow to cool completely to room temperature.

You can use this immediately, but note that the flavour improves over time; the romanesco can be stored in the pickling liquid for up to 2 months in the fridge.

WINE NOTE **A German Riesling from the Mosel would do nicely. Look for** ɟɟ **Prüm.**

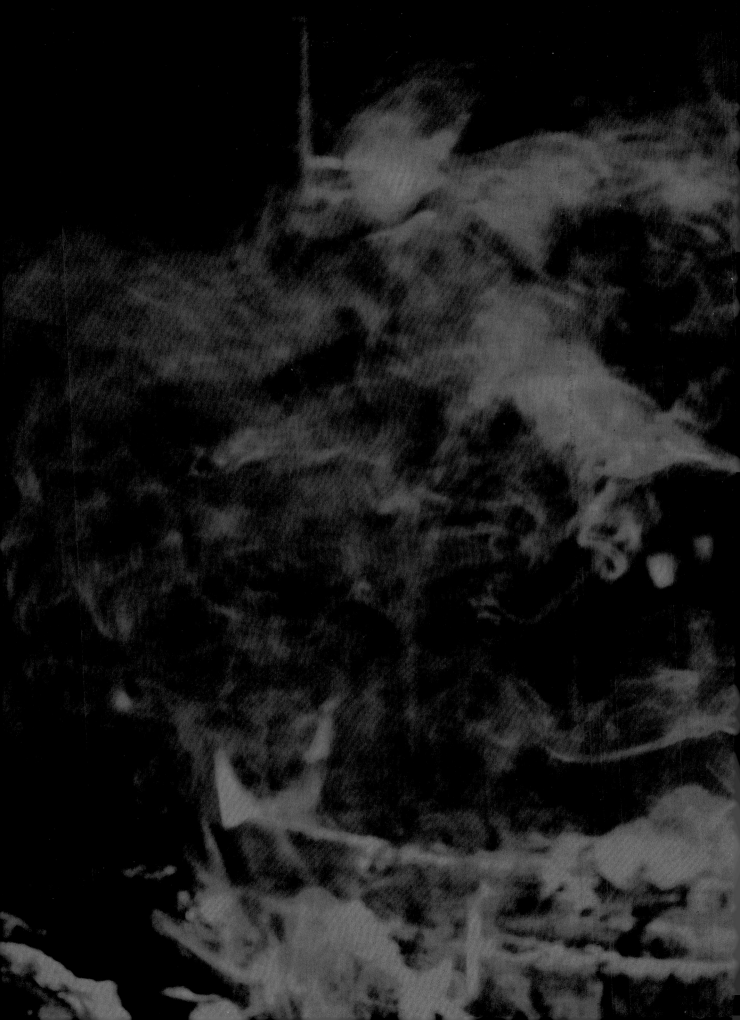

PRIMI

Black trumpet and chanterelle mushrooms — potato gnocchi — parsnips, brown butter and chives

Potato Gnocchi *page 69*

Brown Butter, for finishing *page 219*

4 large parsnips

6 cups (1.5 L) heavy cream

1 cup (250 mL) White Chicken Stock *page 215* or water

1 clove garlic

1 sprig fresh thyme

Canola oil, for deep-frying the parsnip chips

1 ½ Tbsp (22 mL) canola oil, for the mushrooms

½ lb (220 g) fresh black trumpet mushrooms

½ lb (220 g) fresh chanterelle mushrooms

Sea salt and freshly ground black pepper

2 tsp (10 mL) + 2 Tbsp (30 mL) unsalted butter, divided

⅔ cup (160 mL) (approx.) + 1 cup (250 mL) White Chicken Stock *page 215*, divided

2 Tbsp (30 mL) chopped chives, divided

Prepare the gnocchi (including the boiling step) and brown butter.

Peel a very thick layer off all of the parsnips, and separate these peels from the cores. (Peeling the parsnips ensures that the purée is soft, and you will use the peels to make parsnip chips.)

To make the parsnip purée, cut the parsnip cores into 1-inch (2.5 cm) pieces. Place in a medium saucepan with the cream, chicken stock (or water), garlic and thyme. Cover with a cartouche (see the tip on page 95), and bring to a boil. Lower the heat to a gentle simmer, and cook until the parsnips are completely tender.

Remove the pan from the heat, and strain through a coarse sieve, reserving some of the liquid for the purée. Discard the thyme, and place the cooked parsnips and garlic in a blender. Add a little of the reserved liquid, and blend the parsnips to a smooth purée. Push through a fine-meshed sieve and correct the seasoning. Set aside.

To make the parsnip chips, preheat canola oil in a deep fryer to 320°F (160°C). Have ready a large plate or tray lined with paper towels. Then use a vegetable peeler to make the peels into paper-thin strips about 4 inches (10 cm) long. Deep-fry until golden brown, about 5 minutes. Remove from the fryer to drain on the paper towels. The parsnips should be long, thin and crisp. Season with salt and set aside.

Prepare the mushrooms by cleaning off the dirt with a soft brush; you'll have to halve the black trumpets lengthwise to clean the inside of them. Halve the chanterelles, or quarter them if they're especially large.

Continued overleaf

WINE NOTE **An Oregon Pinot Noir would be a perfect pairing.**

Heat the 1 ½ Tbsp (22 mL) canola oil in a medium frying pan. When the oil is hot and almost smoking, add the mushrooms and season with salt and pepper. Cook vigorously for 3 to 4 minutes. Add the 2 tsp (10 mL) butter and cook for a further 30 seconds. Add the ⅔ cup (160 mL) or so of chicken stock so that it covers the bottom of the pan ½ an inch (1 cm) deep, and continue cooking until all of the stock has evaporated and the mushrooms are cooking in the butter, 3 to 4 minutes. Add 1 Tbsp (15 mL) of the chives and set aside.

When ready to serve, warm the parsnip purée.

Put the gnocchi in a wide pot. Add the 1 cup (250 mL) chicken stock, 2 Tbsp (30 mL) butter and a pinch of salt. Cook vigorously until the stock has reduced to one-third of the original volume, 3 to 4 minutes. Add the mushrooms and continue cooking until the stock has almost disappeared, another 2 minutes. Mix in the remaining 1 Tbsp (15 mL) chives.

Spread one-quarter of the parsnip purée over each plate. Spoon over the gnocchi and mushroom mixture. Drizzle 2 Tbsp (30 mL) of the brown butter over each plate, and then scatter a few pieces of the parsnip chips, and serve.

Potato gnocchi — English peas and fava beans, spinach and basil

¼ cup (60 mL) **Basil Pistou** *page 221*

Potato Gnocchi *overleaf*

⅔ cup (160 mL) **fresh fava (broad) beans or edamame** (3½ oz/100 g)

About 4 cups (1 L) **White Chicken Stock** *page 215*

Sea salt

1 ½ **Tbsp** (22 mL) **unsalted butter**

⅔ cup (160 mL) **freshly shelled English peas** (3½ oz/100 g)

1 **handful spinach**

Sea salt and freshly ground black pepper

Freshly grated Parmesan, for finishing

This is a recipe that can easily be made vegetarian by substituting vegetable stock for the chicken.

Prepare the basil pistou.

Prepare the potato gnocchi.

Remove the fava beans from the pods. Have ready a bowl of ice water. Boil the fava beans in salted water for 1 minute, then submerge in the ice water. Peel off the skin off the beans.

Put the gnocchi in a wide pot, and add enough stock to cover by ½ inch (1 cm). Add a pinch of salt and the butter. Bring to a simmer over medium heat.

As soon as the gnocchi starts to simmer, add the peas and continue cooking.

When the stock has reduced to one-quarter of the original volume, the butter has been incorporated and the gnocchi has puffed up, add the fava beans, basil pistou and spinach. Cook until the spinach has wilted and the pistou is coating and sticking to the gnocchi. Correct the seasoning with salt and pepper.

To serve, divide between 4 bowls and grate some Parmesan over the top. *Continued overleaf*

WINE NOTE **Try this dish with a local Chardonnay like Painted Rock or Joie Farm.**

4 large Yukon gold potatoes, about 2 ½ lbs (1.1 kg)

1 egg yolk

½ whole egg, beaten

Sea salt

All-purpose flour *see tip below*

CALCULATING THE AMOUNT OF
FLOUR FOR POTATO GNOCCHI

*Weigh the cooked potatoes that have
been passed through a food mill.
Calculate 75% and 100% of the total
weight; this is the range of how much
flour you'll need:*

WEIGHT of POTATOES	FLOUR 75%	FLOUR 100%
2 lbs (900 g)	**24 oz**	**2 lbs**
	675 g	900 g
	5 ½ cups	7 ½ cups
	1.375 L	1.875 L
2 ½ lbs (1.1 kg)	**30 oz**	**2 ½ lbs**
	825 g	1.1 kg
	7 cups	9 ¼ cups
	1.7 L	2.3 L

*Start with the smaller amount of
flour when making the dough.
If the mixture is too wet and sticky,
add more flour. To test for the right
amount of flour, clean your hands,
and drop a handful of dough.
If there's still dough left on your
palm, you'll need to add more flour.*

Preheat the oven to 400°F (200°C).

Fill a small ovenproof frying pan or baking sheet with salt to a depth of a ½ inch (1 cm). Prick the potatoes all around using a sharp knife, and lay them on the bed of salt. Bake until they're completely tender, about 1 hour. (The salt seasons the potatoes as well as keeps them dry while they bake.)

While still warm, cut in half and scoop out the flesh. Reserve the skin for another use or compost. Pass the flesh through a food mill or potato ricer, or push through a coarse sieve, and set aside to cool. Weigh the potatoes, and calculate the amount of flour you'll need (see note).

Beat the egg yolk and half an egg together. Add to the potato with a good pinch of salt, and beat together until well combined.

Gently fold the flour into the potato, ½ cup (125 mL) at a time, until the dough reaches the right consistency (see tip).

Turn the gnocchi dough onto a floured work surface and gently pull together.

Bring a pot of salted water to a boil.

Divide the dough into 6 pieces. Working with one piece at a time, roll out the dough into ropes that measure 12 × ½ inch (30 × 1 cm). Cut into 1-inch (2.5 cm) pieces.

(At this point, you can freeze the gnocchi you won't be using for the above recipe. You can boil frozen gnocchi straight from the freezer.)

Have ready a large bowl of ice water.

Cook the gnocchi in rapidly boiling water (so the gnocchi is practically jumping out of the water), a handful at a time. When the gnocchi floats to the surface (after about 2 to 4 minutes), count for 30 seconds before removing to the ice bath.

When cool, remove from the ice bath, drain of excess water, dress with olive oil and set aside.

Ricotta gnocchi with rosemary cream — pecorino al tartufo, almond bread crumbs and Piedmont black truffle

Ricotta Gnocchi *below*

Rosemary Cream *overleaf*

Almond Bread Crumbs *overleaf*

About 6 cups (1.5 L) Chicken (or Vegetable) Stock *page 215 (page 217)*

Sea salt

3 Tbsp (45 mL) unsalted butter

Pecorino al tartufo (truffle pecorino), for finishing

¾ oz (20 g) Piedmont black truffle

Start preparing the ricotta gnocchi the day before you want to use it.

Prepare the rosemary cream and the almond bread crumbs and set aside.

Place the gnocchi in a wide pot, and add enough stock to cover by ½ inch (1 cm). Add a pinch of salt and the butter. Bring to a simmer over medium heat, and cook until the butter is incorporated, the stock is reduced to one-quarter of the original volume and the gnocchi has puffed up.

Add the rosemary cream, and simmer until slightly reduced and the sauce clings to the gnocchi.

To serve, divide the gnocchi between 4 bowls. Sprinkle with the bread crumbs, and top with grated pecorino.

Using either a truffle mandolin or microplane, shave one-quarter of the truffle over each plate.

RICOTTA GNOCCHI

1 lb (450 g) ricotta cheese (2 cups/500 mL)

1 egg

2–3 fresh gratings of nutmeg

Sea salt and freshly ground black pepper

1 cup (250 mL) all-purpose flour

2 Tbsp (30 mL) extra virgin olive oil, for dressing gnocchi

Bundle the ricotta in a large piece of cheesecloth, and let it hang over a bowl or pot. Leave it overnight to remove excess liquid.

The following day, place the ricotta in a medium bowl, and beat in the egg, nutmeg and salt and pepper.

Gently work in the flour by cutting in a third at a time until it is all combined. Pull the dough together using your hands, then let it rest for 1 hour in the fridge.

Cut the dough into 6 pieces. Work each piece into a 12 × ½-inch (30 × 1 cm) rope. Cut into 1-inch (2.5 cm) pieces.

Put a pot of salted water on to boil. Have ready a large bowl full of ice water.

Cook the gnocchi a handful at a time in rapidly boiling water (so it is practically jumping out of the water). When the gnocchi floats to the surface (after 2 to 4 minutes), count for 30 seconds before transferring it to the ice bath.

When cool, remove the gnocchi from the ice bath, drain of excess water, dress with olive oil and set aside.

Continued overleaf

ROSEMARY CREAM

4 cups (1 L) heavy cream

2 sprigs fresh rosemary

1 small clove garlic, crushed with back of knife

Pinch of ground nutmeg

In a large pot, combine all of the ingredients, and bring to a boil over high heat. Lower the heat to a simmer, and cook for 15 minutes.

Strain through a fine-meshed sieve to remove the rosemary and garlic and any lumps.

ALMOND BREAD CRUMBS

½ cup (125 mL) panko (Japanese bread crumbs) (1 oz/30 g)

1 tsp (5 mL) olive oil

3 ½ oz (100 g) blanched and peeled almonds (or buy peeled and slivered) (½ cup/125 mL)

1 Tbsp (15 mL) unsalted butter

In a small frying pan, fry the panko in the olive oil for 1 minute.

Add the almonds and butter, and cook until the butter is foaming and the almonds are turning golden brown.

Drain in a colander and transfer to a chopping board. Chop to the consistency of fine bread crumbs.

WINE NOTE Try a white wine from Campania, something with full flavour and body to pair nicely, such as Feudi di San Gregorio Fiano di Avellino.

PASTA

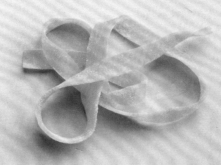

Should you ever have an opportunity to look around a great restaurant's supply shelves, you might be surprised to see dried pasta, such as Di Martino, in the same recognizable box you would find in a high-end Italian grocery store. The fact is, pasta comes in a multitude of shapes and sizes, and each one, both fresh and dried, has a purpose.

Dried spaghetti is perfect for a red sauce, with its capacity for that ideal al dente feel and the ability to spread the sauce around the plate evenly. Take bolognese, for example. We have tried the lighter, summer bolognese and the heavier winter version with both fresh and dried pasta, including tagliatelle. But the best results are with dried spaghetti.

On the other hand, fresh ravioli, filled with house-made ricotta cheese and topped with toasted hazelnuts and some freshly shaved truffle, delivers a silky, melt-in-your-mouth quality that dried pasta simply cannot deliver. We use double-zero-grade flour for our fresh pasta, a grade that is very fine. Good-quality flour has fewer impurities and results in a pasta with a better bite. It took me several years to find the perfect flour to use: Sfoglia Gold Rosa (Farina di Grano Tenero), Grade oo.

CORNERSTONE
INGREDIENT

Casarecce with spicy chorizo sausage — tomato, chili, rosemary and Parmesan

2 Tbsp (30 mL) **olive oil**

1 small red onion, minced

3 lbs (1.4 kg) **chorizo sausage, removed from the casing and crumbled**

1 ½ Tbsp (22 mL) **chopped fresh rosemary**

2 fresh or dried bay leaves

Pinch of dried chili flakes

One 28 oz (796 mL) **can peeled Roma tomatoes, drained and chopped**

Sea salt and freshly ground black pepper

2 cups (500 mL) **dried casarecce pasta** (9 oz/250 g)

½ cup (125 mL) **heavy cream**

4 ½ oz (125 g) **freshly grated Parmesan** (1 ¼ cups/310 mL), **divided**

When you drain cooked pasta, always reserve a bit of the cooking water. It contains some starch from the pasta, and is perfect for thinning your pasta sauce, if necessary.

In a large frying pan, heat the olive oil and fry the onion until golden brown.

Add the sausage, rosemary, bay leaves and chili, and cook over high heat, breaking down the sausage as it cooks. As the fat appears, remove all but 1 Tbsp (15 mL) of it, and continue to cook for 20 minutes.

When the sausage meat is broken down and browned, add the tomatoes, and stir while the mixture returns to the boil. Lower the heat and simmer for 20 minutes, stirring and breaking up the tomatoes. Remove from the heat, and correct the seasoning with salt and pepper.

Bring a pot of salted water to a boil. Cook the pasta until al dente and drain, allowing a little water to cling to the pasta and reserving a bit of the cooking water in the pot in case the sauce needs thinning.

Add the pasta to the chorizo mixture in the frying pan. Add a little of the pasta water, if the mixture is too thick. Stir in the cream and half the Parmesan.

Divide between 4 bowls. Serve with the remaining Parmesan on the side.

WINE NOTE **Pinot Noir from Oregon or a Barbera from Italy would be a good accompaniment.**

Nova Scotia lobster cooked over fire — grilled lemon — spaghetti with fresh tomato and basil

2 ¼ lbs (1 kg) **fresh ripe tomatoes**

10 Tbsp (150 mL) **extra virgin olive oil, divided, for the tomato sauce**

3 cloves **garlic, very thinly sliced**

½ pinch **dried chili flakes**

½ tsp (2.5 mL) **sea salt**

Freshly ground black pepper

2 live **lobsters, 1 ½ lbs (670 g) each**

Sea salt and extra virgin olive oil, for dressing lobsters

2 **lemons, cut in half**

1 lb (450 g) **dried spaghetti**

8 large **fresh basil leaves, torn**

Chopped Italian (flat-leaf) parsley, for garnish

Good-quality olive oil, for finishing

PREPARING LOBSTER

To prepare lobster, bring a large pot of salted water to a boil. Have ready a large bowl full of ice water.

Using a sharp knife, kill the lobster by piercing the back of the head through the cross mark: Find this by laying the lobster on a cutting board (sitting with its underside on the cutting board). You'll see a faint line that runs down the back of the head. Follow this line, and the first line that crosses it is the border between the head and thorax. Push your knife into the X and pull down to the cutting board, cutting the head in half.

Cook the lobster in the boiling water for 2 minutes. Quickly refresh in the ice water to stop the cooking. When cool, drain from the ice water.

While still slightly warm, cut the lobster in half lengthwise, working quickly. Remove the intestinal tract from the tail and the sac from the head. Set aside to cool completely.

For the tomato sauce, cut the whole tomatoes into chunks, then purée in a blender.

Heat 6 Tbsp (90 mL) of the olive oil in a saucepan, and fry the garlic for 2 to 3 minutes, being careful not to brown. Add the chili flakes, followed by the salt and puréed tomatoes. Bring to a brisk boil, and cook until the sauce thickens slightly, roughly 20 minutes. Season with pepper and the remaining 4 Tbsp (60 mL) olive oil, and set aside.

See the tip below on how to prepare the lobster.

Light a wood-fired barbecue, or preheat a gas or charcoal grill or cast-iron grill pan.

Season each lobster with salt, and dress with 1 Tbsp (15 mL) of olive oil. Place on the grill bottom side down, and cook for 2 minutes, and then turn 45 degrees and cook for another 2 minutes. Do the same on the shell side, cooking for 2 minutes, and then turning 45 degrees and cooking for another 2 minutes. Dress with a little more olive oil and set aside.

Cook the lemon halves on the grill for 7 or 8 minutes, or until nicely caramelized.

Meanwhile, bring a pot of salted water to a boil, and cook the pasta until al dente.

Warm the tomato sauce.

Drain the pasta, reserving a little of the cooking water, and dress with olive oil. Add to the tomato sauce, tossing to coat. Add a bit of the pasta water, if the mixture is too thick. Add the basil, and toss again.

To serve, place a spiral of spaghetti on one side of each plate and half a lobster and a piece of lemon on the other side. Sprinkle with chopped parsley, and finish with another drizzle of olive oil.

WINE NOTE **A moderately oaked Chardonnay or a lighter style Pinot Noir is called for.**

TOMATOES

Depending on the weather, the tomato season in
Vancouver runs roughly mid-July to the end of September,
precious little time to enjoy such abundance. Perusing
the shelves of CinCin's larder on an early September day
is a tomato lover's dream. You'll find plenty of heirloom
varieties, including miniature versions. You may even spot
some locally grown San Marzanos, which, with their low
seed and high pulp content, yield a bolognese sauce that
tastes almost as if a wee bit of sugar was added. We have
actually been asked that question, more than once.

Many of the tomatoes used at CinCin come from the
limestone-laced soils at Stoney Paradise, an organic
Kelowna farm owned by Milan Djordjevich, also known
as The Tomato Man. Each week, in season, he arrives at
CinCin to talk fruit with me and to provide a supply of the
most sought-after produce in the region. His legendary
presence at the Saturday Trout Lake farmers' market
elicits a lineup two hours in advance of the market's opening. The quality of these tomatoes eloquently underlines
what *seasonal* really means. ———————————

CORNERSTONE
INGREDIENT

Pappardelle with braised short rib of beef — black pepper, red wine and tomato

1 ½ cups (375 mL) Peposo, with sauce *below*

½ lb (250 g) dried pappardelle pasta

3 Tbsp (45 mL) extra virgin olive oil

3 ½ oz (100 g) freshly grated Parmesan (1 cup/250 mL), plus more for finishing

2 Tbsp (30 mL) chopped Italian (flat-leaf) parsley

Shred the peposo either when it first comes out of the oven (if you made the peposo for this recipe) or after reheating it in a large pot (if you're using leftovers). Break the meat into the sauce and discard the bones.

Bring a large pot of salted water to a boil. Cook the pasta until al dente. Drain, allowing a little water to cling to the pasta and reserving a bit of the cooking water.

Combine the peposo with the pappardelle. Add a little of the pasta water, if the mixture is too thick. Add the olive oil and combine thoroughly. Add the Parmesan and parsley and mix thoroughly.

To serve, divide between 4 bowls and grate over a little more Parmesan.

PEPOSO

¼ cup (60 mL) canola oil

Four ½ lb (220 g) bone-in beef short ribs, about 2 inches (5 cm) thick

Sea salt

2 Tbsp (30 mL) extra virgin olive oil

1 onion, minced

3 cloves garlic, minced

3 Tbsp (45 mL) black peppercorns

2 Tbsp (30 mL) coarsely ground black pepper

1 fresh or dried bay leaf

1 cup (250 mL) red wine

4 cups (1 L) canned peeled San Marzano tomatoes (chopped, with juice)

Preheat the oven to 300°F (150°C).

Heat the canola oil in a large heavy ovenproof sauté pan or pot with a tight-fitting lid. Have ready a wire rack on top of a large plate or tray. Season the meat with salt, and sear it for about a minute on each side until nicely caramelized. Remove from the pan and cool on the wire rack.

Pour off any oil or fat remaining in the pan. Add the olive oil, onion and garlic, and cook until well softened, about 20 minutes.

Add the whole and ground black pepper and the bay leaf, and cook for another minute.

Add the red wine and tomatoes, and bring to a boil.

Return the meat to the pan and lower the heat to a gentle simmer. Cover with a cartouche (see the tip on page 95) and a tight-fitting lid. Bake in the oven for 3 hours, or until the meat is very tender and can be easily pierced with the tip of a knife. Set aside.

WINE NOTE Try a local Syrah or one from Bolgheri, Tuscany.

Linguine with Dungeness crab — lemon, chili and tomato

SERVES 4

2 cups (500 mL) **Tomato Sauce** *below*

1 lb (450 g) **Dungeness crabmeat**

1 ½ **fresh red chilis, seeded and minced**

Juice of 2 lemons

1 ½ **cloves garlic, ground to a paste with a little salt**

½ cup (125 mL) **olive oil**

1 ½ **handfuls Italian (flat-leaf) parsley, finely chopped, divided**

½ lb (220 g) **dried linguine**

Good-quality olive oil, for finishing

Prepare the tomato sauce.

Pick through the crabmeat to remove pieces of shell, and place the crab in a medium bowl. Add the chilis, lemon juice and garlic. Stir in the olive oil. The sauce should be quite liquid. Add half the parsley and stir in.

Bring a large pot of salted water to a boil.

Place the crab mixture into a large frying pan and warm gently.

In a separate saucepan, heat the tomato sauce.

Cook the linguine until al dente. Drain, allowing a little water to cling to the noodles and reserving a bit of the cooking water.

Add the linguine to the crab mixture, and warm gently. Add the tomato sauce and an extra drizzle of olive oil. Add a little of the pasta water, if the mixture is too thick.

Divide between 4 bowls, sprinkle with the remaining parsley and serve.

TOMATO SAUCE Makes 6 cups (1.5 L)

5 **cloves garlic, very thinly sliced**

½ cup (125 mL) **extra virgin olive oil**

Pinch of dried chili flakes

Two 28 oz (796 mL) **cans peeled San Marzano tomatoes, whole**

2 tsp (10 mL) **sea salt**

Freshly ground black pepper

In a large saucepan, fry the garlic in the oil until it just starts to colour. Strain out and discard the garlic.

Stir the chili flakes into the oil. Add the tomatoes, salt and a few grinds of pepper.

Cook at a brisk simmer until thickened, about 1 hour.

Pass the tomatoes through a food mill, or push through a coarse sieve.

WINE NOTE **A rosé from the Okanagan, such as Tightrope 2014, will work nicely with this dish.**

Parmesan, potato and rosemary mezzaluna — salsa verde — olive oil

Salsa Verde *page 220*

1 recipe Pasta Dough *overleaf*

Mezzaluna Stuffing *overleaf*

Semolina flour, for dusting

Olive oil, for the cooked mezzaluna

Sea salt, for the cooked mezzaluna

Freshly grated Parmesan, for finishing

Prepare the salsa verde (ideally the day before so that the flavours have time to blend), pasta dough and mezzaluna stuffing.

Divide the pasta dough into 4 pieces. Using a pasta machine, roll out each piece to the thinnest possible setting. A good test is to be able to read a newspaper through the dough.

Dust a baking sheet or tray with semolina, and have more of it on hand.

Dust the work surface with semolina and lay out the 4 sheets of dough. The long side of the rectangle should be facing you (see photo on page 86).

Fill a piping bag with the stuffing. For each sheet, pipe eight 1 Tbsp (15 mL) rounds of the filling onto the dough along the centre of the pasta sheet, about 1 inch (2 cm) apart.

Moisten the edges of the dough using cold water and a pastry brush. Fold the dough over the filling from the edge nearest to the edge farthest away. The fold of the pasta should be against the edge of the filling. Press the dough together and press out any air pockets that may have formed. Cut out semicircles or *mezzalunas* (half moons) using a pastry cutter. Set aside on the prepared tray.

Bring a large pot of salted water to a boil. Drop the mezzalunas into the water, and cook for 4 minutes. To avoid overcrowding, cook in 3 batches.

Drain the mezzalunas, place in a bowl or pan, drizzle with olive oil and add a pinch of salt.

To serve, divide between 4 plates, spoon over some of the salsa verde and grate a little Parmesan over the top.

Continued overleaf

WINE NOTE With this dish we pair Ca'Rugate Monte Alto Soave 2009. If you can't find it, look for a Soave Classico.

You can use all-purpose flour instead of pasta flour, but it's a poor substitute. The "00" pasta flour should be readily available. Make the pasta dough ahead, and let it rest while you prepare the other components of the recipe. You can even make it the night before.

PASTA DOUGH

2 cups (500 mL) "00" pasta flour
(we prefer Pivetti) (9 oz/250 g)

2 whole eggs

3 egg yolks

½ tsp (2.5 mL) olive oil

In a food processor, blend the flour.

Whisk together the whole eggs. Using a scale, measure out exactly 3 ⅜ oz (95 g) of the whole eggs. In a small bowl, whisk together the egg yolks, and add exactly 1 ¾ oz (50 g) of the egg yolks to the whole eggs. (Save the rest of the egg for another use, or compost it.) Mix to combine, and whisk in the olive oil.

With the food processor running at high speed, add the egg mixture in a slow, steady stream. Blend until the mixture has the texture of bread crumbs.

Turn out onto a work surface, and knead until the dough becomes silky and smooth, about 8 minutes. Roll into a ball. Using a knife, cut an X into the surface. Wrap in plastic wrap and place in the fridge to rest for 1 hour before use.

MEZZALUNA STUFFING

1 large Yukon gold potato (9 oz/250 g)

¼ cup (60 mL) unsalted butter

1 Tbsp (15 mL) chopped fresh rosemary

1 egg yolk

1 ¾ oz (50 g) freshly grated Parmesan
(½ cup/125 mL)

½ cup (125 mL) grated Piave Vecchio cheese
(if not available, use more Parmesan)
(1 ¾ oz/50 g)

Sea salt and freshly ground black pepper

Preheat the oven to 400°F (200°C).

Fill a small ovenproof frying pan or baking sheet with salt to a depth of a ½ inch (1 cm). Prick the potato all around using a sharp knife, and lay it on the bed of salt. Bake until it's completely tender, about 1 hour. (The salt seasons the potato as well as keeps it dry while it bakes.)

While still warm, cut in half and scoop out the flesh. Reserve the skin for another use or compost. Pass the flesh through a food mill or potato ricer, or push through a fine-meshed sieve, and set aside to cool.

In a small frying pan, melt the butter and warm it until it foams. Add the rosemary, and fry, removing the pan from the heat before it colours.

Combine the cooled potato with the rosemary and butter, as well as the egg yolk, Parmesan and Piave. Season with salt and pepper.

Ravioli of ricotta and Parmesan — summer truffle from Umbria, parsley and roasted hazelnuts

SERVES 4

1 recipe **Pasta Dough** *page 86*

2 cups (500 mL) **Ricotta Filling** (18 oz/500 g) *facing page*

3 oz (85 g) **toasted and skinned hazelnuts** (½ cup/125 mL), **crushed** *see tip below*

½ cup (125 mL) **Truffle Vinaigrette** *facing page*

Semolina flour, for dusting

Olive oil

Sea salt

4 good pinches chopped Italian (flat-leaf) parsley, for finishing

Freshly grated Parmesan, for finishing

¾ oz (20 g) **Italian summer truffle**

TOASTING HAZELNUTS

To prepare the hazelnuts, preheat the oven to 425°F (225°C). Toast in a baking sheet until golden brown, about 7 to 8 minutes. When cool enough to handle, rub in a hand towel to remove the skin. Break into pieces using a rolling pin.

Prepare the pasta dough, ricotta filling, toasted hazelnuts and truffle vinaigrette.

Divide the pasta dough into 4 pieces. Using a pasta machine, roll each piece out to the thinnest possible setting. A good test is to be able to read a newspaper through the dough.

Dust a baking sheet or tray with semolina, and have more of it on hand.

Dust the work surface with semolina, and lay out the 4 sheets of dough. The long side of the rectangle should be facing you.

Place the Ricotta Filling in a piping bag. For each sheet, pipe eight 1 Tbsp (15 mL) rounds of the filling onto the dough along one side of the pasta sheet, about 1 inch (2.5 cm) apart (see photo on page 86).

Moisten the edges of the dough using cold water and a pastry brush. Fold the dough over the filling starting with the nearest edge. Press the dough together and press out any air pockets that may have formed. Cut through the pasta between each ravioli, and trim the edges. Set the ravioli aside on the prepared tray.

Bring a pot of salted water to a boil. Drop the ravioli into the water, and cook for 4 minutes. If necessary, cook the ravioli in 2 or 3 batches to avoid overcrowding.

Drain and place in a bowl or pan, drizzle with olive oil and add a pinch of salt.

To serve, divide the ravioli between 4 plates, drizzle with truffle vinaigrette, sprinkle with hazelnuts and parsley and grate some Parmesan over the top. Using either a truffle mandolin or microplane, shave one-quarter of the truffle over each plate.

1 lb (450 g) **ricotta cheese** (2 cups/500 mL)

3 ½ oz (100 g) **freshly grated Parmesan** (1 cup/250 mL)

2 fresh gratings of nutmeg

Sea salt and freshly ground black pepper

4 egg yolks

Put the ricotta, Parmesan and nutmeg into the bowl of an electric mixer. Using the paddle attachment, beat the cheeses together. Add a good pinch of salt and 2 grinds of black pepper.

With the machine running at moderate speed, add the eggs one at a time. After each addition, turn off the machine and scrape the bowl. Season with salt and pepper.

TRUFFLE VINAIGRETTE

1 Tbsp (15 mL) **Dijon mustard**

1 ½ Tbsp (22 mL) **white wine vinegar**

¾ tsp (4 mL) **balsamic vinegar**

½ Tbsp (22 mL) **honey**

Sea salt

½ cup (125 mL) **neutral oil (canola, sunflower, grapeseed)**

1 ½ Tbsp (22 mL) **walnut or hazelnut oil**

1 ½ Tbsp (22 mL) **truffle oil (preferably black truffle)**

Sea salt and freshly ground black pepper

Place the mustard, both vinegars and honey in a stainless steel bowl (or any bowl that won't take on the odour of the truffle), and add a pinch of salt. Whisk together.

Pour the oils into the bowl, and stir the ingredients together. Season with salt and pepper.

WINE NOTE **Antinori makes the perfect wine for this: Castello della Sala Cervaro 2011.**

TRUFFLES

Truffles show up on our menu for at least three-quarters of the year, whether they're white (Alba), black (Burgundy and Périgord) or summer truffles, depending on the season. We mostly get them from Italy, with some from France and Spain, transported in special FedEx courier jets that carry delicate, time-sensitive cargo.

We use truffles for both meat and fish dishes, and in pasta, gnocchi and risotto, shaving the truffle over the dish. The trimmings go in butter, vinaigrettes, stocks, pasta stuffing and sauces. To infuse eggs, store a white (Alba) or black (Périgord) truffle inside the egg carton (with the eggs) for a couple days. The aroma infuses through the eggshell. To infuse butter, place the butter in a container, wrap the truffle in a kitchen towel on top of it, and seal the container for a couple days.

In November, CinCin hosts Festa del Fungo, an annual truffle and mushroom festival. The highlight of the month is a multi-course dinner that stars truffles in every dish.

A truffle doesn't have a lot of actual flavour, surprisingly. It's all contained in the *aroma*, unmistakably accentuating any dish, filling the senses and enhancing the appetite. —————

CORNERSTONE
INGREDIENT

Ravioli of fire-cooked squash — brown butter, sage and hazelnuts — fresh Toscano pecorino

SERVES 4

1 recipe Pasta Dough *page 86*

Squash Filling *below*

1 cup (250 mL) Brown Butter *page 219*

3 oz (85 g) toasted and skinned hazelnuts (½ cup/125 mL) *see tip on page 88*

20 fresh sage leaves

Canola oil, for deep-frying sage leaves

Olive oil, for the cooked ravioli

Sea salt

7 oz (200 g) soft, unaged Toscano pecorino (if unavailable, use Parmesan), for finishing

Prepare the pasta dough, squash filling, roasted hazelnuts and brown butter. To make the ravioli, follow the instructions for assembling and shaping the ricotta ravioli (page 88), substituting the squash filling.

Have ready a small plate lined with a paper towel. To prepare the sage leaves, preheat canola oil in a deep fryer or small heavy-bottomed pot to 300°F (149°C). Pick the sage leaves from their stems, leaving about ¼ inch (6 mm) of the stem intact. Drop the leaves into the fryer, and cook until they float on top of the oil and it stops bubbling, about 45 seconds. Drain on the paper towel.

Bring a pot of salted water to a boil. Drop the ravioli into the water, and cook for 4 minutes. If necessary, cook in 3 batches to avoid overcrowding the pot. Drain and place in a bowl or pan. Drizzle over some olive oil and add a pinch of salt.

To serve, divide the ravioli between 4 plates. Dress with the brown butter. Sprinkle 2 Tbsp (30 mL) of hazelnuts over each plate. Grate over some of the pecorino and finish with 5 sage leaves. Serve.

SQUASH FILLING

One 2 ¼ lb (1 kg) squash (red kuri or Hokkaido would be ideal)

1 Tbsp (15 mL) olive oil

Sea salt and freshly ground black pepper

2 Tbsp (30 mL) unsalted butter

1 small red onion, minced

1 clove garlic, minced

½ nutmeg, freshly grated

½ bunch fresh marjoram

½ pinch dried chili flakes

½ lb (220 g) mascarpone (1 cup/250 mL)

2 ¾ oz (75 g) freshly grated Parmesan (¾ cup/185 mL)

The squash can also be fire-cooked in the coals. Once the squash skin turns black, put it beside the coals and cook for an hour.

Preheat the oven to 425°F (220°C).

Cut the squash into 6 pieces, and remove the seeds. Place on a baking sheet, brush with the olive oil and season with salt and pepper. Cook in the oven until soft and a knife cuts through very easily, about 1 hour and 45 minutes.

When cool enough to handle, scrape the flesh from the skin. Let it sit in a colander to drain any excess liquid. Pass the flesh through a food mill or push it through a coarse sieve, and set aside.

Heat the butter in a medium frying pan, and fry the onion until soft. Add the garlic, nutmeg, marjoram and chili. Cook just long enough to allow the flavours to blend. Add the squash, mix thoroughly and cool.

When cold, beat in the mascarpone and Parmesan. Correct the seasoning.

WINE NOTE For a special occasion, crack open a bottle of Querciabella Batàr 2012, and for everyday drinking, Altesino Bianco 2013.

Risotto of lobster from Nova Scotia — sunchoke and Piedmont black truffle

½ recipe **Risotto Base** *page 214*

Sunchoke Chips *facing page*

Sunchoke Purée *facing page*

1 live **lobster, 1 ½ lbs** (670 g)

1 cup (250 mL) **White Chicken Stock** *page 215*

Sea salt

¼ cup (60 mL) **unsalted butter**

3 ½ oz (100 g) **finely grated fresh Parmesan** (1 cup/250 mL)

1 Tbsp (15 mL) **chopped chives**

¼ oz (7 g) **Piedmont black truffle**

Prepare the risotto base (if you don't have it on hand).

Prepare the sunchoke chips and purée.

To prepare the lobster, bring a large pot of salted water to a boil. Have ready a large bowl full of ice water.

Follow the directions on page 77 (see tip) for preparing the lobster, up until boiling it.

Twist and remove the claws and arms in one piece.

Cook the body in the boiling salted water for 4 minutes. Quickly refresh in the ice bath to stop the cooking. (Keep the pot on the stove.) Working quickly, while still slightly warm, cut the lobster in half lengthwise and remove the tail meat. Remove the intestinal tract from the tail and the sac from the head. Cut the tail meat into bite-sized pieces.

Blanch the claws and arms in the boiling water for 1 minute. Quickly refresh in the ice bath. Working quickly, while still slightly warm, remove the flesh from the shell and cut into bite-sized pieces.

Combine the risotto base in a large pot with the stock and a pinch of salt. While stirring, bring to a simmer over moderate heat. Cook until the stock has reduced to one-third of the original volume, 3 to 4 minutes.

Remove from the heat, and add the sunchoke purée. Return to the heat, and cook for 1 more minute.

Remove from the heat, and add the lobster meat, butter, Parmesan and chives. Stir together until thick, creamy and fully combined, and the lobster is just warmed through. Check the seasoning.

Divide between 4 bowls, sprinkle with the Sunchoke Chips, grate the truffle over the top and serve.

SUNCHOKE CHIPS

6 sunchokes (Jerusalem artichokes)

Canola oil, for deep-frying

Sea salt

Peel the sunchokes. Using a mandolin or sharp knife, slice them crosswise very finely. Rinse under cold running water for 15 minutes. Drain and pat dry.

Have ready a large plate or tray lined with paper towels. Preheat canola oil in a deep fryer to 320°F (160°C). Fry the sunchokes in batches until crisp and golden brown. Drain on the paper towels, and season with salt.

SUNCHOKE PURÉE

1 lb 10 oz (750 g) sunchokes, peeled and thinly sliced

1 cup (250 mL) whole milk

½ cup (125 mL) heavy cream

½ cup (125 mL) water

1 sprig fresh thyme

1 clove garlic, crushed with back of knife

Sea salt

Put all of the ingredients in a pot, and cover with a cartouche (see the tip below). Bring to a boil, lower the heat to a gentle simmer and cook very slowly until the sunchokes can be easily pierced with a knife, about 30 minutes.

Drain the mixture through a sieve or colander, retaining the liquid. Remove the sprig of thyme, and place the cooked sunchokes and garlic in a blender.

Purée the mixture, adding enough of the liquid to achieve a stiff purée.

MAKING A CARTOUCHE

A cartouche is a piece of parchment or grease-proof paper that sits on top of the liquid inside your pot to cover the food and keep it submerged as it cooks. When cutting the parchment, turn your pot upside down and trace around it, or trace around the lid.

WINE NOTE **Vintage Champagne, if you're feeling flush, and a local or California Chardonnay for everyday drinking.**

Buy fava beans in the pod when they're in season; if you can't get them, you can use edamame. This dish is designed so it can easily be made vegetarian. Simply use vegetable stock in place of chicken.

Green risotto — English peas, fava beans and spinach

½ recipe **Risotto Base** *page 214*

¼ cup (30 mL) **Basil Pistou** *page 221*

⅔ cup (160 mL) **fresh fava (broad) beans or edamame** (3½ oz/100 g)

1 cup (250 mL) **White Chicken Stock** *page 215*

Sea salt

⅔ cup (160 mL) **freshly shelled English peas** (3½ oz/100 g)

1 handful **spinach**

¼ cup (60 mL) **unsalted butter**

3½ oz (100 g) **finely grated fresh Parmesan** (1 cup/250 mL)

1 Tbsp (15 mL) **chopped Italian (flat-leaf) parsley**

1 Tbsp (15 mL) **chopped chives**

Prepare the risotto base and the basil pistou (if you don't have them on hand.)

Remove the fava beans from the pods. Have ready a bowl of ice water. Boil the fava beans in salted water for 1 minute, then submerge in the ice water. Peel the skin off the beans.

Place the risotto base in a large pot. Add the stock and a pinch of salt. Over moderate heat, bring the risotto to a simmer, stirring with a spoon.

As soon as the risotto starts to simmer, add the English peas. Cook until the stock has reduced to one-third of the original volume.

Remove from the heat and add the fava beans and spinach.

Return to the heat and cook for a further 1 minute.

Remove from the heat and add the butter, Parmesan, parsley, chives and pistou. Stir together until it appears rich, creamy and fully combined. Check the seasoning.

Divide between 4 bowls and serve.

WINE NOTE We like to pair this dish with a Piedmont Chardonnay, such as Elio Grasso Educato or Pio Cesare L'Altro.

Risotto of smoked Haida Gwaii sablefish — maple vinegar, honey and mustard — herb and young vegetable leaves

½ recipe Risotto Base *page 214*

⅓ cup (80 mL) **Maple Vinegar, Honey and Mustard Vinaigrette** *below*

1 cup (250 mL) **White Chicken Stock** *page 215*

Sea salt

2 oz (60 g) **smoked sablefish (or other smoked fish)**

¼ cup (60 mL) **unsalted butter**

3 ½ oz (100 g) **finely grated fresh Parmesan** (1 cup/250 mL)

2 Tbsp (30 mL) **chopped chives**

4 small handfuls **herb and young vegetable leaves (carrot tops, young beet greens, celery leaves)**

Prepare the risotto base (if you don't have it on hand) and the vinaigrette.

In a large pot, combine the risotto with the stock and a pinch of salt over moderate heat. While stirring, bring to a simmer. Cook until the stock has reduced to one-third of the original volume.

Remove from the heat and add the sablefish. Return to the heat and cook for a further 2 minutes.

Remove from the heat and add the butter, Parmesan and chives. Stir together until fully combined. Check the seasoning.

To serve, divide between 4 bowls and drizzle over the vinaigrette. Sprinkle with the herbs and young vegetable leaves.

PREPARING SMOKED SABLEFISH

Place the sablefish trimmings onto a perforated tray. Shovel embers from a hot fire onto a separate tray. Put the perforated tray (with the trimmings) on top of the tray with coals, and cook the fish for 20 minutes. Transfer the cooked fish to a wide pot and barely cover with milk (about 2 inches). Add 1 stem of parsley, 1 stem of thyme, 1 bay leaf and 6 black peppercorns. Heat until the milk begins to simmer, then turn off the heat and let the fish cool in the liquid. Remove the fish from the milk and flake it over the risotto.

MAPLE VINEGAR, HONEY AND MUSTARD VINAIGRETTE

3 Tbsp (45 mL) **Dijon mustard**

3 Tbsp (45 mL) **olive oil**

3 Tbsp (45 mL) **maple vinegar**

1 tsp (5 mL) **honey**

Lightly whisk all ingredients together.

WINE NOTE **Try a local Riesling, like Synchromesh, or a G.D. Vajra Riesling from Piedmont.**

RISOTTO

Called "the king of rices," carnaroli rice, with its high starch content and long grains, is usually a chef's first choice for making risotto. (The two other notable types are arborio and vialone nano.) This is certainly true for me; I prefer Acquerello il Riso, which is aged for a year.

Seasonal ingredients make for some splendorous variations, including a memorable, brilliant-green stinging-nettle version that leaves you longing for seconds. The quintessential Veneto dish of saffron risotto, known as risotto Milanese, is served at CinCin with a braised veal shank, drawing the Mediterranean right to the table.

The key with risotto, even when prepared with the more commonly available arborio rice, is to cook it slowly, gradually adding broth to the rice as it absorbs it, which is why the resulting dish is so redolent of flavours. The additions, such as nettles, or, classically, mushrooms, come near the end, with freshly grated Parmesan or Grana Padano and a little butter. Surely there is no better comfort food than risotto. —————————

CORNERSTONE
INGREDIENT

Wood-grilled Alaskan sea scallops — risotto of stinging nettles

SERVES 4

½ recipe **Risotto Base** *page 214*

6 Tbsp (90 mL) **Stinging Nettle Pistou** *below*

3 Tbsp (45 mL) **Lemon Oil** *page 223*

1 cup (250 mL) **White Chicken Stock** *page 215*

Sea salt

11 oz (310 g) **scallops** (3 per person)

Extra virgin olive oil, for dressing scallops

¼ cup (60 mL) **unsalted butter**

3 ½ oz (100 g) **finely grated fresh Parmesan** (1 cup/250 mL)

4 small handfuls herb and young vegetable leaves (carrot tops, young beet greens, celery leaves) (optional)

Prepare the risotto base (if you don't have it on hand).

Prepare the stinging-nettle pistou and lemon oil.

Place the risotto base in a large pot. Add the stock and a pinch of salt. Over moderate heat, bring the risotto to a simmer, stirring with a spoon. Cook until the stock has reduced to one-third of the original volume, 3 to 4 minutes. Remove from the heat.

Meanwhile, prepare the scallops. Light a wood-fired barbecue, or preheat a gas or charcoal grill or cast-iron grill pan. Dress the scallops with olive oil and season with salt. Grill for 4 minutes, turning 3 times. Set aside at room temperature.

When the risotto stock has reduced, add the butter, Parmesan and pistou, and combine thoroughly. Check the seasoning and add salt to taste.

To serve, divide the risotto between 4 bowls. Place 3 scallops on top of each risotto, and drizzle with lemon oil. Finish with a scattering of herb and vegetable leaves.

STINGING NETTLE PISTOU   Makes 2 cups (500 mL)

4 cloves **garlic**

5 oz (140 g) **stinging nettles**

7 oz (200 g) **freshly grated Parmesan** (2 cups/500 mL)

1 ¼ cups (310 mL) **extra virgin olive oil**

Sea salt and freshly ground black pepper

Cut the cloves of garlic in half lengthwise, and remove the germ.

Put a pot of water on to a boil, and have ready a bowl full of ice water.

Wear gloves to protect your hands, and remove the stinging nettle leaves from the stems.

Plunge the nettle leaves into the boiling water for 30 seconds, then remove to the ice bath. When the leaves are cool, squeeze them dry and chop roughly (they will no longer sting at this point).

Combine the garlic, nettles, Parmesan and olive oil in a blender. Start the machine on a low setting, then increase the speed, blend until smooth. Season with salt and pepper. Store in a sealed container in the fridge for up to 2 weeks.

WINE NOTE Vermentino from Sardinia, please!

Spaghetti al ragù — 6-hour bolognese, veal and pork with pancetta, Parmesan

6 oz (170 g) **unsalted butter** (¾ cup/185 mL)

½ cup (125 mL) **extra virgin olive oil**

4 medium **carrots, diced**

5 stalks **celery, diced**

2 medium **onions, minced**

8 cloves **garlic, minced**

½ lb (220 g) **pancetta, finely chopped**

Sea salt

2 ¼ lb (1 kg) **ground pork**

2 ¼ lb (1 kg) **ground veal**

3 cups (750 mL) **white wine**

5 cups (1.25 L) **whole milk**

4 cups (1 L) **canned peeled San Marzano tomatoes, drained and chopped**

2 cups (500 mL) **White Chicken Stock** *page 215*

Freshly ground black pepper

1 lb (450 g) **dried spaghetti**

Unsalted butter, for finishing

Freshly grated Parmesan, for finishing

In a large pot, heat the butter and oil over medium. Add the carrots, celery, onions, garlic and pancetta. Add a pinch of salt and cook for 15 minutes, stirring occasionally.

Turn up the heat to high, and add the pork and veal, breaking up the lumps with a spoon.

When the mixture starts to brown, add the wine, and cook until it has completely evaporated.

Add the milk, tomatoes and stock. Check the seasoning, and add pepper and more salt, if necessary. Cook at a gentle simmer for 6 hours, or until the sauce is thick and oily.

Bring a pot of salted water to a boil. Cook the pasta until al dente. Drain, allowing a little water to cling to the pasta and reserving a bit of the cooking water.

Add the pasta to the bolognese, thinning the sauce with a little pasta water, if necessary, along with a good spoonful of butter to finish.

To serve, divide between 4 bowls, and offer Parmesan to sprinkle over the top.

WINE NOTE At the restaurant we pair this with Vietti La Crena Barbera. A local Pinot Noir would do nicely as well.

SECONDI

Alberta beef tenderloin — potatoes with prosciutto and Parmesan — ash-roasted onions — salmoriglio

Ash-Roasted Onions *overleaf*

Salmoriglio, for finishing *page 221*

Potato, Prosciutto and Parmesan Gratin *overleaf*

Sea salt and freshly ground black pepper

2 stalks collard greens

Four 5 oz (140 g) beef tenderloin steaks or one 1 ¼ lb (570 g) piece of beef tenderloin

Olive oil, for dressing tenderloin and sautéing collards

2 cups (500 mL) White Chicken Stock *page 215*

2 cloves garlic, minced

Good-quality olive oil, for finishing

Prepare the ash-roasted onions. (They take 2 hours to roast, and can be prepared up to a week in advance.)

Prepare the salmoriglio the day before, and prepare the gratin either the day before or on serving day.

On serving day, light a wood-fired barbecue, or preheat a gas or charcoal grill or cast-iron grill pan, for the onions and the beef.

To grill the roasted onions, remove the outer skin and tough outer layers. Quarter them, liberally dress with olive oil and season with salt and pepper. Grill until nicely charred and coloured. Keep warm.

Reheat the gratin, if it's not still hot.

Put a medium pot of salted water on to boil, and have ready a large bowl of ice water. Strip the collard greens from their stems, reserving the stems. Cut each stem and leaf half in 2 (or more if they are very big pieces). Blanch in the boiling water for 5 minutes, or until just tender. Refresh in the ice bath. Drain and pat dry.

Season the beef with a drizzle of olive oil and salt and pepper. Place on the preheated grill, and cook for 5 minutes. Turn and cook for another 5 minutes. Turn again and cook for 2 minutes. Turn again and cook for a further 2 minutes. (The total cooking time is 14 minutes.) Let it rest for at least 7 minutes.

Meanwhile, in a frying pan, sauté the collard greens in olive oil with the garlic, a pinch of salt and a grind of black pepper. Immediately add the chicken stock, and cook on high heat until the stock has evaporated, 2 to 3 minutes.

To serve, place each steak on a plate along with some onion, collards and a spoonful of the gratin. Dress with the salmoriglio. Add a drizzle of olive oil and serve.

Continued overleaf

WINE NOTE At the restaurant, we serve this dish with Carpineto Farnito Cabernet Sauvignon 2009. At home, a Tuscan or Californian Cabernet Sauvignon would substitute perfectly.

ASH-ROASTED ONIONS

2–3 whole onions, skin intact

Olive oil, for dressing

Salt and freshly ground black pepper

You can also roast the onions whole in the oven, but then you lose the most important flavours of this dish.

The ideal preparation is to use a previous fire or barbecue. As the firewood or coals burn, throw the whole onions in the bed of the fire/coals with their skins on. Cook the onions in the coals until nicely charred and tender, about 2 hours.

Can be kept in the fridge for a week.

POTATO, PROSCIUTTO AND PARMESAN GRATIN

2 cups (500 mL) heavy cream

1 sprig fresh thyme

1 whole clove garlic, peeled

6 large Yukon gold potatoes, peeled and cut into ⅛-inch (3 mm) slices

4 full slices prosciutto (full length of the prosciutto), ¹⁄₁₆–⅛ inch (2–3 mm) thick, cut in half

7 oz (200 g) finely grated fresh Parmesan (2 cups/500 mL)

Put the cream in a small saucepan with the thyme and garlic. Warm and allow the flavours to infuse for about 30 minutes.

Preheat the oven to 450°F (230°C).

Butter 4 small ovenproof dishes (ours are 6 inches/15 cm square).

Start with a layer of potatoes in the base of the dish, then a layer of prosciutto, then a sprinkling of Parmesan. Repeat until you have 3 layers of potato and 2 layers of prosciutto, finishing with potato and a sprinkling of Parmesan.

Strain the infused cream over the gratin, cover with foil and bake for 1 hour, or until the potatoes can be pierced easily with a knife.

Remove the foil and bake uncovered for a further 15 minutes.

Remove from the oven and set aside.

"Crazy water"—or acqua pazza in Italian— is usually broth made with by-catch or fish that otherwise did not sell.

Acqua pazza — Arctic char in crazy water, saffron and chili

SERVES 4

Clams *overleaf*

Vegetable Minestrone *overleaf*

Chili Oil, for finishing *page 222*

Four 5 oz (140 g) **Arctic char fillets, skin on**

Sea salt

1 Tbsp (15 mL) **canola oil**

3 Tbsp (45 mL) **unsalted butter (at CinCin, we use Brown Butter** *page 219*)**, divided**

4 handfuls spinach (chop large leaves in half)

1 Tbsp (15 mL) **chopped Italian (flat-leaf) parsley**

1 Tbsp (15 mL) **chopped chives**

Prepare the clams, and then the minestrone (the minestrone uses the juice from cooking the clams). Prepare the chili oil if you don't have it on hand.

Season the char with sea salt. Heat a nonstick frying pan and coat with the canola oil. When the oil is hot, add the char, skin side down. Cook until the skin is golden brown and crispy, 4 to 5 minutes. Flip over the fish and cook for 1 minute. Add 1 Tbsp (15 mL) of the butter to the pan and swirl it around. Remove the pan from the heat, and let stand uncovered in a warm place for 5 minutes, allowing the fish to cook in the residual heat.

Meanwhile, melt another 1 Tbsp (15 mL) butter in a wide sauté pan and add the spinach. Season evenly with salt and toss around, cooking until the spinach wilts.

Combine the minestrone with the shelled and unshelled clams, and reheat with the remaining 1 Tbsp (15 mL) butter. Bring to a boil and check the seasoning. Add the parsley and chives.

To serve, divide the clams and vegetables between 4 bowls. Place a spoonful of spinach in the centre of each bowl on top of the vegetables. Place a piece of fish on top of the spinach, skin side up, and drizzle with chili oil. *Continued overleaf*

WINE NOTE If you're in the mood for a red wine, look for an Oregon Pinot Noir. If you prefer white, a local Chardonnay will do the trick.

3 Tbsp (45 mL) **olive oil**

3 medium **shallots, thinly sliced**

1 head **garlic, cut through horizontally
(cloves kept together and unpeeled)**

2 sprigs **fresh thyme**

2 ¼ lbs (1 kg) **fresh clams**

1 cup (250 mL) **white wine**

8 cups (2 L) **White Chicken Stock** *page 215*
(or enough to barely cover clams)

Heat the olive oil in a large wide pot, and sweat the shallots, garlic and thyme until tender, about 5 to 8 minutes.

Add the clams, and turn the heat up high. Cover the pot, and shake repeatedly to help open the clams.

When the clams start to open, add the white wine, replace the lid and continue cooking and shaking the pot over high heat.

When the clams are fully open, add enough chicken stock to barely cover. Replace the lid and bring to a boil.

When the pot comes to a boil, remove from the heat. Remove the clams from the broth, spreading them on a baking sheet to cool.

Strain the broth through a fine-meshed sieve or cheesecloth. Return to a boil and reduce by half. Reserve for use in the vegetable minestrone.

Pick through the clams. Leave half in the shell and remove the meat from the remaining half. Discard the empty shells. Set the clams aside while you prepare the minestrone and char.

1 Tbsp (15 mL) **canola oil**

1 Tbsp (15 mL) **extra virgin olive oil**

1 small or ½ medium **onion, minced**

1 clove **garlic, minced**

8 medium **carrots, cut into ½-inch** (1 cm) **dice**

4 stalks **celery, cut into ½-inch** (1 cm) **dice**

Sea salt

Clam juice (from Clams recipe above)

Pinch of saffron

2 **leeks, white part only, cut into ½-inch**
(1 cm) **dice**

Heat the canola and olive oils in a large, wide pot. Add the onion and garlic, cover and cook gently for about 10 minutes, being careful not to brown.

When soft, add the carrots and celery, and cook gently for a further 10 minutes, seasoning the vegetables with salt as they cook.

Add the strained clam juice, and bring to a boil. Add saffron, lower the heat to a gentle simmer and cook for 5 minutes.

Add the leeks and cook for 5 more minutes. Remove from the heat and cool.

Albacore tuna grilled over alder — gigante beans, Tyee spinach, basil pesto and olive oil

2 cups (500 mL) **Giant White Beans** *page 153*

¼ cup (60 mL) **Basil Pesto (aggressively seasoned, with strong garlic)** *page 220*

Four 5 oz (140 g) **pieces sushi-grade albacore tuna** (or two 10 oz/285 g pieces)

Sea salt and freshly ground black pepper

Extra virgin olive oil, for dressing tuna

3 Tbsp (45 mL) **unsalted butter**

4 handfuls Tyee or regular spinach

16 Nocellara del Belice (or Castelvetrano) olives, pitted and halved

Good-quality olive oil (not too spicy), for finishing

Prepare the white beans and the pesto, and set aside.

Remove the tuna from the fridge, and bring to room temperature (about 20 minutes).

Light a wood-fired barbecue, or preheat a gas or charcoal grill or cast-iron grill pan.

Season the tuna with salt and pepper, and dress with a thin coating of olive oil.

Cook the tuna on the hot grill for at least 1 minute on each side, 4 minutes maximum in total, turning it to create an attractive criss-cross pattern. The tuna should remain rare in the centre. Remove from the grill and let rest for at least 3 minutes.

Place the beans in a sauté pan or medium saucepan with enough of the cooking liquid to cover by ½ inch (1 cm). Add a pinch of salt and the butter. Bring to a boil, lower the heat to a simmer and cook for about 3 to 4 minutes, until reduced to one-quarter of the original volume.

Add the spinach and continue cooking until it starts to wilt. Mix in the pesto and olives. Check the seasoning and adjust if necessary.

To serve, divide the bean mixture into 4 bowls. Cut the tuna into thin (¼-inch/6 mm) slices and spread over the beans. Season the cut side with salt and pepper, and drizzle over a little olive oil.

WINE NOTE Try a local Pinot Blanc from Blue Mountain or St. Innocent Pinot Blanc from Oregon.

Whole grilled branzino — sea salt and garlic roast Sieglinde potatoes — Swiss chard, leaves and stems

Garlic, Rosemary and Sea Salt Roast Potatoes
page 160

Sautéed Swiss Chard *page 152*

4 branzino (European sea bass), 1 lb (450 g) **each, gutted, gills removed and thoroughly cleaned**

Olive oil, for dressing branzino and for finishing

Sea salt

2 lemons, halved

Prepare the roast potatoes and the Swiss chard.

Light a wood-fired barbecue, or preheat a gas or charcoal grill or cast-iron grill pan.

Make 4 incisions on each side of the branzino, cutting from head to tail through the skin and halfway into the flesh. Dress with olive oil and season with salt on both sides and in the cavity.

Put the branzino and lemons on the barbecue: Cook the branzino for about 16 minutes, turning 4 times throughout, until nicely charred and cooked through. Cook the lemon for about 7 to 8 minutes, or until nicely caramelized, turning the lemon 90 degrees halfway through to get good grill marks. Allow the fish to rest for at least 5 minutes.

While the fish is cooking, reheat the chard and potatoes.

To serve, place the fish and lemon on one side of each plate and the vegetables on the other. Drizzle with a little olive oil before serving.

WINE NOTE **Try a local Chardonnay like Blue Mountain.**

Chargrilled chicken with harissa — couscous two ways — golden raisins, rapini and soffritto — olive oil and lemon

Classic Vinaigrette, for the couscous (2 tsp/10 mL) and for finishing *page 222*

Couscous with Golden Raisins *overleaf*

Toasted Couscous *overleaf*

¼ cup (60 mL) Soffritto *page 213*

2 bunches rapini (about 20 stems)

4 lemons, quartered

Juice of 2 lemons

2 ¼ lbs (1 kg) granulated sugar

Sea salt and freshly ground black pepper, to taste

8 cups (2 L) water

2 sprigs fresh rosemary

10 sprigs fresh thyme, divided

1 fresh or dried bay leaf

24 cloves garlic, unpeeled

One 3 ½ lb (1.6 kg) chicken cut into 8 pieces (2 thighs, 2 drumsticks, each breast cut in half)

Extra virgin olive oil, for dressing chicken

1 Tbsp (15 mL) harissa paste

5 Tbsp (75 mL) extra virgin olive oil, divided

2 Tbsp (30 mL) unsalted butter

Eight 3-inch (8 cm) sticks cinnamon

Prepare the classic vinaigrette, the 2 kinds of couscous and the soffritto.

Light a wood-fired barbecue, or preheat a gas or charcoal grill or cast-iron grill pan closer to the cooking time (while the chicken drains).

Bring a pot of salted water to a boil. Have ready a large bowl full of ice water. Cook the rapini until just tender, about 4 minutes. Submerge in the ice water to cool. Drain, pat dry and set aside.

In a large pot, combine the lemon quarters, lemon juice, sugar, salt and pepper, water, rosemary, 2 sprigs of the thyme, bay leaf and garlic, and bring to a boil.

Immediately lower the heat to a gentle simmer, add the chicken drumsticks and thighs and cook for 15 minutes.

Add the breasts and cook for a further 10 minutes. Remove from the heat, and let cool in the stock for about 5 minutes.

Remove the chicken pieces from the stock, and drain on paper towels. Reserve the lemon pieces and garlic, and discard the stock.

Dress the chicken with a little olive oil, and season with salt and pepper. Cook on the preheated grill, turning every few minutes to cook evenly, 4 to 5 minutes in total.

Remove the chicken from the grill, and spread a little harissa paste over each piece.

Heat 2 Tbsp (30 mL) of the olive oil and butter in a sauté pan. Add the cinnamon and the remaining 8 sprigs of thyme along with the lemon pieces and garlic from the stock. Cook until nicely caramelized, about 2 minutes.

Continued overleaf

WINE NOTE Try a beautiful Pinot Noir from Oregon called Angela. Choose a Pinot Noir from 2012, a stellar year. If you're in the mood for white, try a Tuscan Chardonnay.

In a separate sauté pan, heat the remaining 3 Tbsp (45 mL) olive oil, and add the cooked rapini with a pinch of salt. Cook for 2 minutes. Add the soffritto and cook for a further 2 minutes, or until the rapini and soffritto start to stick to the bottom of the pan. Remove from the heat.

Reheat the couscous.

To serve, spoon some of the couscous mixture into the middle of each plate. Arrange 2 pieces of chicken on top along with the garlic, lemon, thyme and cinnamon sticks. Scatter over 4 pieces of the rapini and soffritto, and drizzle with vinaigrette.

COUSCOUS WITH GOLDEN RAISINS

1 Tbsp (15 mL) **golden raisins**

½ cup (125 mL) **couscous** (3 ½ oz/100 g)

½ tsp (2.5 mL) **salt**

1 ½ tsp (7.5 mL) **olive oil**

½ cup (125 mL) **boiling water, for the couscous**

Zest of ½ **lemon**

2 tsp (10 mL) **fresh lemon juice**

2 tsp (10 mL) **Classic Vinaigrette** *page 222*

1 Tbsp (15 mL) **chopped fresh mint**

Place the raisins in a bowl. Pour boiling water over them to cover by 2 times their volume. Cool to room temperature, and drain off the water.

Put the couscous, salt and olive oil in a nonreactive bowl. Pour over the ½ cup (125 mL) boiling water, stir and quickly cover with plastic wrap. Allow to stand for 13 minutes.

Fluff the couscous with a fork. Mix in the lemon zest and juice, vinaigrette, mint and soaked raisins.

TOASTED COUSCOUS

2 tsp (10 mL) **unsalted butter**

1 ¼ cups (310 mL) **toasted couscous (you can buy it toasted)** (9 oz/250 g)

2 cups (500 mL) **water**

Sea salt

Melt the butter in a small saucepan. Stir in the couscous, and immediately add the water and salt and turn the heat to high. When the mixture comes to a boil, lower the heat to a very gentle simmer, cover and cook for 12 minutes.

Remove from the heat, and transfer the couscous to a large nonreactive bowl. Fluff with a fork and season to taste with salt.

Combine with the other couscous and keep warm.

Duck with Richmond corn cooked in embers — polenta and crispy broccoli — duck sauce

½ recipe Soft Polenta *page 166*

⅔ cup (160 mL) Lamb/Duck Sauce, using duck bones *page 218*

2 heads broccoli, trimmed, cut into florets

4 cobs corn, husks attached

Four ½ lb (220 g) boneless duck breasts

Sea salt and freshly ground black pepper

3 Tbsp (45 mL) canola oil, divided

Canola oil, for deep-frying broccoli

About ½ cup (125 mL) semolina flour, for dusting and dredging

2 Tbsp (30 mL) unsalted butter

Good-quality olive oil, for finishing

Prepare the polenta, but use a 9 × 13-inch (23 × 33 cm) rimmed baking sheet instead. Follow the steps until you let it set for 3 hours. Then cut the polenta into 4 discs that are about 2 ½ inches (6 cm) in diameter. (You will have leftover polenta.)

Prepare the duck sauce.

Bring a pot of salted water to a boil. Have ready a large bowl full of ice water. Cook the broccoli until just tender, about 3 minutes. Dunk in the ice water to cool. Drain and pat dry.

Light a wood-fired barbecue or charcoal grill, or have at hand a gas flame at a low temperature.

When the wood is white or the barbecue coals are glowing red or smouldering white, add the corn with the husks attached directly in the fire/coals. Cook until the husks are nicely charred. If using a gas flame, hold the corn over the low gas flame to achieve the same result. When cool enough to handle, remove the husks. Using a sharp knife, remove the corn kernels from the cob, and set aside.

Preheat the oven to 425°F (220°C).

Trim the duck breasts of any sinew or silver skin. Season liberally on both sides with salt and pepper.

Heat 1 Tbsp (15 mL) canola oil in a heavy ovenproof sauté pan. Place the duck in the pan, skin side down, over moderate heat. Allow the pan to build heat slowly, rendering fat from the skin and occasionally draining the excess fat from the pan.

When the skin on the breast is golden brown and a little crispy, place the pan in the oven and cook for 8 minutes. Have ready a wire rack on top of a large plate or tray. Remove duck from the oven, turn the breast onto its flesh side and return to the oven to cook for a further 3 minutes. Remove from the oven, take the duck from the pan and let rest on the wire rack for at least 5 minutes.

While the duck is cooking, fry the polenta. Heat the remaining 2 Tbsp (30 mL) canola oil in a large ovenproof nonstick frying pan. When the oil is hot, carefully place the polenta cakes into the pan. When the edges just start to turn golden brown, place the pan in the oven. Cook for 5 minutes, flip the polenta over and return to the oven to cook for a further 3 minutes. Remove from the oven.

Preheat canola oil in a deep fryer to 360°F (182°C). Dust an 11 × 17-inch (28 × 43 cm) baking sheet with semolina. Have ready a large plate or tray lined with paper towels. Dredge the broccoli florets in the semolina, shake off the excess and fry in the hot oil until golden brown. Drain on the paper towels and season with salt.

Heat the butter in a frying pan, and lightly sauté the corn, seasoning with a little salt.

To serve, heat the duck sauce. Place a polenta cake on one side of each plate. Slice the duck breast across the grain, and place on the opposite side of the plate, seasoning the cut side with a little salt. Spread the corn over the duck and polenta, and spoon over some of the duck sauce. Place at least 4 of the broccoli florets on each plate, and drizzle with a little olive oil.

WINE NOTE **Try this dish with an Okanagan Pinot Noir like Spierhead or Liquidity.**

*We use spring salmon in the spring and coho later in the year,
but you can use whatever is fresh and available. Leftover poached
tomatoes are delicious on their own or on toast.*

Pacific salmon — Sungold tomatoes poached in olive oil, fennel-onion confit, basil

SERVES 4

¼ cup (60 mL) **Fennel-Onion Confit** (7 oz/200 g) *page 155*

½ lb (220 g) **Olive Oil–Poached Cherry and Sungold Tomatoes** *overleaf*

¼ cup (60 mL) **Basil Pistou, for finishing** *page 221*

Four 5 oz (140 g) **salmon fillets, skin on**

Sea salt

1 Tbsp (15 mL) **canola oil**

1 Tbsp (15 mL) **unsalted butter (at CinCin, we use Brown Butter** *page 219***)**

12 **black olives, pitted and halved**

¼ cup (60 mL) **chopped Italian (flat-leaf) parsley**

2 Tbsp (30 mL) **chopped chives**

Prepare the fennel-onion confit, the cherry and sungold tomatoes and the basil pistou, and set aside. (Note that the confit takes 2 hours to cook.)

Remove the salmon from the fridge, and slowly bring to room temperature (allow about 20 minutes). Season the fish on both sides with salt.

Heat the canola oil in a nonstick frying pan over moderate heat. When the pan is almost smoking, slide the fish into the pan, skin side down. Cook for 5 minutes or until the skin becomes golden brown and crisp. Flip the fish over and cook on its flesh side for 2 minutes. Add the butter to the pan, and swirl around. Remove the pan from the heat, and let stand uncovered in a warm place for 5 minutes, allowing the fish to cook in the residual heat.

Reheat the fennel-onion confit, and stir in the olives, parsley and chives.

Reheat the cherry and Sungold tomatoes.

To serve, spread 1 Tbsp (15 mL) of the Basil Pistou on each plate. Place 1 Tbsp (15 mL) of the confit in the centre. Spoon the tomatoes around the confit and on top of the pistou. Place a piece of fish on top of the fennel, skin side up. *Continued overleaf*

WINE NOTE **Salmon and Pinot Noir are a perfect pairing. Go with local, Oregon or Burgundy for a splurge.**

OLIVE OIL-POACHED CHERRY AND SUNGOLD TOMATOES

½ cup (125 mL) olive oil

3 medium shallots, minced

1 clove garlic, minced

1 lb (450 g) mixed cherry and Sungold tomatoes

1 Tbsp (15 mL) each chopped fresh chives, basil, tarragon and Italian (flat-leaf) parsley

Sea salt

Heat the olive oil in a medium saucepan. Add the shallots and garlic, and cook slowly until very soft and almost translucent, being careful not to brown.

Add the tomatoes and cook gently. When the skins start to split and the tomatoes start to wilt and release their juice, remove from the heat and let it cool to room temperature. (This will keep nicely in the fridge for 2 to 3 weeks, especially if you keep it covered in olive oil.)

To finish, reheat gently to just above room temperature, mix in the herbs and season to taste with salt. (The tomatoes have a fuller flavour served warm rather than hot.)

OLIVE OIL

It is hard to imagine a more quintessential Mediterranean ingredient than olive oil. Neolithic people harvested olives in the Mediterranean basin as far back as the eighth century BC.

Today, as then, the oil extracted has numerous applications, most commonly as cooking oil. Spain produces nearly 45 percent of the world supply, while Italy produces only 22 percent. Perhaps surprisingly, Italy is a net importer of olive oil. Olive oils come in a wide range of qualities, with cold-pressed extra virgin oils taking the top tier. Flavours vary wildly, from green grass and freshly mown hay to spicy, ground black pepper notes.

CinCin keeps oils on hand from both Italy and Spain. Italian wineries often press their own oil, and CinCin uses Villa Cafaggio oil, as well as having the estate's wines on its list. From Spain, Deortegas and Cladium are the oils of choice.

We use several different oils in different applications throughout the menu. But surprisingly little is used for cooking, as the aroma and flavour can change when heated. Most is for dressing or finishing salads and select dishes.

A great olive tapenade and two types of house-made breads for dipping are presented at each table. Hard to be more traditional than that—or more delicious.

CORNERSTONE
INGREDIENT

Halibut from Haida Gwaii — crosnes, sunchokes and Brussels sprout leaves — mushroom essence, olive oil

4 cloves Whole Roasted Garlic, peeled and crushed *page 163*

⅔ cup (160 mL) Mushroom Essence, for finishing *page 219*

1 oz (30 g) crosnes or Chinese artichokes

12 sunchokes (Jerusalem artichokes)

1 head garlic, cut through horizontally (cloves kept together and unpeeled)

1 sprig fresh thyme

1 sprig Italian (flat-leaf) parsley

Sea salt

4 ½ lbs (2 kg) Sieglinde (German butter) potatoes, peeled and cut into 1 ½-inch (4 cm) pieces

2 cups (500 mL) heavy cream

½ lb (220 g) unsalted butter (1 cup/250 mL)

Four 5 oz (140 g) halibut fillets, skin on

7 Tbsp (105 mL) canola oil, divided

Clarified unsalted butter, for dressing halibut

20 Brussels sprouts

1 tsp (5 mL) + 2 Tbsp (30 mL) unsalted butter, divided

¾ oz (20 g) black trumpet mushrooms (about 6), halved and insides lightly brushed of dirt

5 Tbsp (75 mL) finely chopped chives

Freshly ground black pepper

Good-quality olive oil, for finishing

Prepare the roasted garlic and mushroom essence if you don't already have these on hand.

Bring a pot of salted water to a boil. Have ready a bowl of ice water. Clean the crosnes and cook them until just tender, about 6 minutes. Submerge in the ice water to cool. Drain, pat dry and set aside.

Place the sunchokes, garlic, thyme, parsley and salt in a heavy-bottomed pot. Pour in enough cold water to cover by 2 inches (5 cm), and bring to a boil. Lower the heat to a gentle simmer, and cook until just tender. Turn off the heat, and allow the sunchokes to cool in the pot. Remove from the pot, discarding the cooking liquid. Cut the sunchokes in half lengthwise, and set aside.

Place the potatoes in a pot with a good pinch of salt and enough water to cover by 2 inches (5 cm). Bring to a boil, then lower the heat to a gentle simmer. Cook until tender and easily pierced with the tip of a knife. Drain off the water and return the potatoes to a low heat. Cook slowly for about 10 minutes, allowing excess moisture to evaporate and shaking the pot occasionally (do not stir).

Meanwhile, in a small saucepan, bring the cream to a boil and remove from the heat.

Pass the potatoes through a food mill or potato ricer or push them through a coarse sieve into a clean frying pan or sauté pan. Put the pan over low heat, and beat in the 1 cup (250 mL) butter and the crushed roasted garlic. Beat in the cream a little at a time. Transfer to a bowl and keep warm. Clean the pan.

Continued overleaf

Continued overleaf

WINE NOTE Pinot Noir if you're in the mood for red, or go with a fuller-style white wine.

Preheat the oven to 425°F (220°C).

Season the fish with salt. Heat a large ovenproof non-stick frying pan, and add 2 Tbsp (30 mL) of the canola oil. Place the fish in the pan, skin side down. Cook until the skin starts to caramelize, then move to the oven for 6 minutes. Flip the fish over and drizzle with a little clarified butter. Return the pan to the oven for a further 3 minutes. Remove from the oven, and let stand uncovered in a warm place for 5 minutes, allowing the fish to cook in the residual heat.

Meanwhile, remove the outer leaves from the Brussels sprouts and discard. Separate the remaining leaves and set them aside. Heat a frying pan with 1 Tbsp (15 mL) of the canola oil. When the oil smokes, add the leaves, which should crackle and colour. Add a pinch of salt and the 1 tsp (5 mL) of unsalted butter.

Heat 2 frying pans, and add 2 Tbsp (30 mL) of canola oil to each.

In 1 pan, lightly sauté the mushrooms, finishing with 1 Tbsp (15 mL) of butter, the chives and a grind of pepper.

In the other pan, fry the sunchokes until golden brown and crispy, finishing with 1 Tbsp (15 mL) of butter. Season with salt.

Warm the mushroom essence.

To serve, spread some of the potato purée over one side of each plate. Spoon some of the crosnes and sunchokes over the other side. Place the fish on top of the vegetables, and sprinkle the mushrooms and Brussels sprouts over the plate. Finally, drizzle with mushroom essence and a small amount of olive oil.

Sablefish from the Hecate Strait — chickpeas, chili, spinach and piquillo peppers

SERVES 4

Four 6 oz (170 g) **pieces sablefish (Alaskan black cod)**

Canola oil, for searing the fish

Sea salt

1 Tbsp (15 mL) **clarified unsalted butter**

One 19 cz (540 mL) **can chickpeas** (or 2 cups/500 mL cooked)

2 cups (500 mL) **White Chicken Stock** *page 215*

2 good pinches dried chili flakes

5 Tbsp (75 mL) **unsalted butter**

⅔ cup (160 mL) **fresh New Zealand spinach (stems and leaves)**

3 piquillo peppers, cut into strips (if not available, use roasted red peppers)

Good-quality olive oil, for finishing

Remove the sablefish from the fridge, and slowly bring to room temperature (about 20 minutes).

Preheat the oven to 425°F (220°C).

Heat an ovenproof nonstick frying pan over moderate heat, and add a drizzle of canola oil. Season the fish on both sides with salt. When the pan is almost smoking, slide in the fish, skin side down, and cook until the skin starts to caramelize.

Move the pan to the oven, and cook the fish for 5 minutes, or until the skin becomes golden brown and crisp.

Flip the fish over, return to the oven and cook on the flesh side for 2 minutes. Remove from the oven, add the clarified butter and swirl it around. Let stand uncovered in a warm place for 5 minutes, allowing the fish to cook in the residual heat.

Meanwhile, place the chickpeas in a medium pot with the chicken stock, a pinch of salt, the chili flakes and the ⅓ cup (80 mL) butter. Bring to a boil, and cook rapidly until the stock has reduced to one-quarter of the original volume.

Add the spinach and peppers, and continue cooking until the stock has reduced by half. Correct the seasoning and finish with a grind of pepper.

To serve, divide the chickpea mixture between 4 bowls, and finish with a drizzle of olive oil. Place the fish on top.

WINE NOTE **A German or local Riesling will complement this dish nicely.**

Wood-grilled Alberta lamb rack — tomatoes roasted on the vine — baba ganoush and pesto — polenta alla griglia, lamb sauce

SERVES 4

½ recipe Polenta alla Griglia, cut into 4 pieces *page 165*

6 Tbsp (90 mL) Baba Ganoush *overleaf*

6 Tbsp (90 mL) Basil Pesto *page 220*

½ cup (125 mL) Lamb/Duck Sauce, using lamb bones *page 218*

2 Tbsp (30 mL) extra virgin olive oil

24 small tomatoes on the vine

Sea salt and freshly ground black pepper

3 Tbsp (45 mL) balsamic vinegar

Cornmeal, for dusting polenta

4 racks of lamb, 3 bones per rack

Canola oil, for dressing lamb

Good-quality olive oil, for finishing

The day before serving, prepare the polenta, following the steps until you spread it and leave it to cool overnight. Prepare the baba ganoush, the pesto and the lamb and duck sauce anytime beforehand.

Preheat the oven to 425°F (210°C).

Heat a medium ovenproof frying pan over moderate heat. Add the olive oil and tomatoes and cook for about a minute, seasoning with salt and pepper.

As soon as the tomatoes start to sizzle, move the pan to the oven, and roast until the skins just start to split. Remove from the oven, add the balsamic vinegar and cool to room temperature. Leave the oven on.

Light a wood-fired barbecue, or preheat a gas or charcoal grill or cast-iron grill pan.

Cut the polenta into 4 pieces. Dust the polenta pieces in cornmeal, and grill. When nicely coloured and warmed to the centre, set aside.

Season the lamb with salt and pepper, and dress with canola oil. Have ready a wire rack on top of a large plate or tray. Grill lamb, turning frequently from the fat side to the bone side and to the edges. Cook until the meat is nicely marked and cooked to a medium temperature, 20 to 25 minutes. Cool on the wire rack for 5 to 8 minutes.

Meanwhile, warm the lamb sauce in a small pot and warm the tomatoes, polenta and eggplant in the hot oven.

To serve, spread some of the baba ganoush and the pesto on opposite sides of 4 plates. Top with the hot tomatoes and polenta. Cut the lamb into individual chops, and arrange around the vegetables. Season the cut side of the meat with a little salt, and pour over some of the sauce. Drizzle each plate with olive oil.

Continued overleaf

WINE NOTE **This wine needs a Cabernet Sauvignon like Carpineto Farnito.**

2 cloves **Whole Roasted Garlic (taken from a full head)** *page 163*

2 **globe eggplant**

1 **Tbsp** (15 mL) **tahini (sesame paste)**

10 **Tbsp** (150 mL) **extra virgin olive oil**

½ **tsp** (2.5 mL) **smoked paprika**

Lemon juice to taste

Sea salt and freshly ground black pepper

Olive oil, for finishing

Prepare the roasted garlic confit.

Light a wood-fired barbecue or a gas flame. Place the whole eggplant in the burning coals of the barbecue, or using a pair of tongs hold the eggplant over the gas flame.

Cook the eggplant until the outer skin becomes dark and scorched and the centre is tender. If the outer skin is blackened but the centre is still firm, wrap the eggplant in foil. Preheat the oven to 350°F (180°C) and cook until the centre becomes tender.

Remove from the oven, carefully open the foil and let the eggplant cool enough to be able to peel off the skin. Roughly chop the flesh, then place it in a blender. Add the tahini, olive oil, garlic confit and smoked paprika, and blend until smooth.

Pass the purée through a tamis or fine-meshed sieve. Season with salt, pepper and lemon juice.

Serve at slightly warmer than room temperature, drizzled with olive oil.

Red-wine-braised short rib of beef — braised carrots and cannellini beans

Four ½ lb (220 g) bone-in beef short ribs, about 1 inch (2.5 cm) thick

2 large whole carrots

1 leek, white part only, cut into 3 to 4 pieces

2 medium onions, peeled and halved

5 whole cloves garlic, peeled

8 sprigs Italian (flat-leaf) parsley

4 sprigs fresh thyme

2 fresh or dried bay leaves

12 cups (3 L) red wine

1 cup (250 mL) canola oil, divided

Sea salt and freshly ground black pepper

All-purpose flour, for dusting short ribs

8 cups (2 L) White Chicken Stock *page 215*, divided

One 14 oz (398 mL) can cannellini (or white gigante) beans (or 1 ½ cups/375 mL cooked)

1 Tbsp (15 mL) unsalted butter

2 Tbsp (30 mL) chopped Italian (flat-leaf) parsley

The day before you plan to serve the dish, marinate the ribs. First, divide each rib into about 4 pieces, cutting between the bones (but keeping the meat on the bones).

Place in a large nonreactive bowl. Place the carrots, leeks, onions and garlic over the top, followed by the parsley, thyme and bay leaves. Pour in the wine, cover and place the bowl in the fridge and marinate overnight.

The following day, drain the wine from bowl, reserving the wine. Pat the meat and vegetables dry, and reserve the aromatics (garlic, parsley, thyme and bay leaves) as well.

Preheat the oven to 300°F (150°C).

Strain the red wine through a fine-meshed sieve, place in a pot and slowly bring to a boil. Remove the scum as it floats to the surface. Simmer for about 30 minutes, or until reduced by half, and then strain through cheesecloth.

Heat ¼ cup (60 mL) of the canola oil in a large frying pan. Have ready a wire rack on top of a large plate or tray. Season the meat with salt and pepper, and dust with flour (you can skip dusting the meat with flour, if you have gluten allergies). Sear on all sides (about 1 minute each side) until deep golden brown. Place on the wire rack to drain the excess oil.

Using the remaining ¾ cup (185 mL) canola oil, cook the reserved vegetables in the same pan until golden brown, 15 to 20 minutes. Drain in a colander.

Continued overleaf

WINE NOTE This is a dense, heavy dish, so we need a wine that can hold its own. Amarone will pair well and be able to match the rich flavours.

In a large ovenproof pot, combine the meat, vegetables, reserved aromatics and wine reduction. Add enough stock to cover. Place a cartouche (see the tip on page 95) over the meat to keep it below the surface of the liquid, and bring to a simmer.

Move to the oven and braise for about 3 hours, or until the meat is falling from the bone.

Allow the meat to rest in the pot for 2 hours, then remove to a wire rack.

Strain the liquid into a medium saucepan through a fine-meshed sieve. Retain the carrots, and discard the other vegetables and aromatics. Reduce the liquid to a sauce consistency (about one-quarter of the original volume), about 45 minutes.

Trim the carrots into neat, bite-sized pieces.

Put the meat in a wide ovenproof sauté pan or baking dish, and add the reduced sauce and the carrots. Place in the oven to warm through.

Rinse and strain the cannellini beans. Place in a pot with barely enough chicken stock to cover, a pinch of salt and the butter. Cook vigorously until the stock has evaporated and butter is coating the beans. Add the chopped parsley, and check the seasoning.

Remove the meat from the oven, and divide the ribs and carrots between 4 plates. Spoon the cannellini beans over the ribs and serve.

Wood-grilled loin of venison — red cabbage and parsnips — gnocchi Romani and red wine

SERVES 4

½ recipe **Braised Red Cabbage** *overleaf*

Red Wine Sauce *overleaf*

4 pieces (½ recipe) **Gnocchi Romani** *page 164*

4 parsnips

Four 5 oz (140 g) **pieces venison (or elk) loin, cleaned of sinew**

Extra virgin olive oil, for dressing venison

Sea salt and freshly ground black pepper

Canola oil, for deep-frying parsnips

Good-quality olive oil, for finishing

The day before serving, start preparing the cabbage.

Prepare the red wine sauce and the gnocchi. For the gnocchi, follow the steps until you've shaped the gnocchi and put them in the fridge to set for 30 minutes.

For the parsnips, put a medium pot of salted water onto a boil. Peel and cut each parsnip lengthwise into quarters. Cut in half horizontally to create 8 pieces. Cook until very tender, or until they can be crushed easily between 2 fingers when squeezed. Drain on paper towels and cool completely.

Light a wood-fired barbecue, or preheat a gas or charcoal grill or cast-iron grill pan.

Dress the venison with a little olive oil, and season liberally with salt and pepper. Have ready a wire rack on top of a large plate or tray. Grill venison, turning frequently on all sides and edges. Cook until the meat is nicely marked and cooked to medium-rare, about 8 to 10 minutes. Remove from the grill, and place on the wire rack to rest for at least 5 minutes.

Meanwhile, preheat the canola oil in a deep fryer to 325°F (160°C). There should be enough oil to cover the parsnips by 2 inches (5 cm). Have ready a large plate or tray lined with paper towels. Fry the parsnips until crisp and brown. Drain on the paper towels, and keep warm.

Follow the baking instructions for the gnocchi (page 164), using a smaller baking sheet.

Warm the red cabbage and the wine sauce.

To serve, place the cabbage on one side of each plate and the gnocchi on the other. Slice the venison into ¼-inch-thick (6 mm) pieces, season with salt and pepper and place between the cabbage and gnocchi. Drizzle over a little wine sauce. Arrange the parsnips attractively over the plate, then drizzle with a little olive oil.

Continued overleaf

WINE NOTE **Try a Chianti Classico Riserva or a Brunello.**

BRAISED RED CABBAGE

1 ¾ lbs (800 g) **red cabbage** (1 small cabbage)

1 Tbsp (15 mL) **granulated sugar**

3 Tbsp (45 mL) **red wine vinegar**

Sea salt, to taste

2 Tbsp (30 mL) **extra virgin olive oil**

1 ½ cups (375 mL) **thinly sliced red onion** (7 oz/200 g)

½ cup (125 mL) **raisins**

1 cup (250 mL) **red wine vinegar**

½ cup (125 mL) **port**

3 slices **unpeeled ginger**

½ Tbsp (7.5 mL) **dried juniper berries** (omit if not available)

The day before serving the venison, quarter the cabbage and remove and discard the core. Shred the quarters into slices about ¼ inch (6 mm) thick.

In a large bowl, combine the cabbage with the sugar, vinegar and salt. Marinate overnight.

The following day, preheat the oven to 350°F (180°C).

Heat the olive oil in an ovenproof rondeau or frying pan, and gently fry the onion for about 15 minutes, being careful not to brown. Add the marinated cabbage and raisins. Deglaze with the red wine vinegar by pouring it in and cooking until it has almost evaporated. Do the same with the port. Add the ginger and juniper.

Place the pan in the preheated oven, cover and cook the cabbage for about 1 ½ hours, or until tender. Stir well and correct the seasoning. Remove the ginger and juniper.

Keeps for up to a month in a sealed container in the fridge.

RED WINE SAUCE   Makes 1 1/2 cups (375 mL)

2 Tbsp (30 mL) **unsalted butter**

1 large **shallot,** sliced

1 sprig **fresh thyme**

6 **white peppercorns,** crushed

⅔ cup (160 mL) **red wine**

1 cup (250 mL) **Reduced Brown Chicken Stock**
page 216

Sea salt and freshly ground black pepper

Melt the butter in a medium pot. Add the shallot, thyme and crushed peppercorns. Cook slowly until deep golden and rich in colour, about 30 minutes.

Add the red wine and reduce to one-third of the original volume.

Add the reduced stock and reduce a little, until the sauce coats the back of a spoon.

Pass through a fine-meshed sieve.

Keeps for up to 2 weeks in a sealed container in the fridge.

Veal osso buco — saffron risotto, gremolata

6 veal shins (also called veal shanks; ask the butcher to cut the shin 1 ½ inches (4 cm) thick, across the bone)

Sea salt and freshly ground black pepper

All-purpose flour, sifted, for dusting veal shin

¼ cup (60 mL) canola oil

4 oz (110 g) unsalted butter (½ cup/125 mL)

1 small red onion, minced

2 cloves garlic, minced

1 celery heart (tender centre stalk), finely chopped

½ cup (125 mL) white wine

4 sprigs fresh thyme

2 cups (500 mL) canned peeled San Marzano tomatoes, drained and chopped

1 fresh or dried bay leaf

Saffron Risotto *overleaf*

Gremolata *overleaf*

Preheat the oven to 325°F (160°C).

Season the veal with salt and pepper, and dust with flour (you can skip dusting the meat with flour, if you have gluten allergies).

Heat some of the canola oil in a large heavy ovenproof sauté pan with a lid over medium heat. Have ready a wire rack on top of a large plate or tray. Brown the meat all over, 2 pieces at a time so as not to lose heat in the pan through overcrowding. After about 4 to 5 minutes in total, when the meat is nicely browned and caramelized on all sides, set aside on the wire rack to drain any excess fat. Repeat with the remaining oil until all the meat is seared.

Clean the pan, then use it to heat the butter over medium heat. Add the onion, garlic and celery, and cook for about 20 minutes, or until very soft. Pour in the wine and simmer to reduce by half, about 10 to 15 minutes.

Return the veal to the pan on top of the vegetables. Add the thyme, tomatoes and bay leaf. The liquid in the pan should come halfway up the pieces of veal. If it doesn't, add more wine. Bring to a boil and remove from the heat. Cover with a cartouche (see tip on page 95) and a lid, and cook in the oven for 3 to 3 ½ hours, until the meat comes away from the bone easily and can be pierced without resistance. Let it rest for 30 minutes before serving.

Meanwhile, make the gremolata and the risotto.

To serve, divide the veal and sauce between 4 plates. Divide the saffron risotto between the 4 plates, placing it beside the veal, and sprinkle the gremolata on top.

Continued overleaf

WINE NOTE This is a Piedmont classic and calls for a classic Piedmont wine like G.D. Vajra Albe Barolo or Vietti Perbacco.

SAFFRON RISOTTO

Pinch of saffron threads (1 g) or powder (2 g)

5 cups (1.25 L) **White Chicken Stock** *page 215* **or Vegetable Stock** *page 217*

2 Tbsp (30 mL) **canola oil**

2 Tbsp (30 mL) **unsalted butter**

1 small onion, minced

1 small clove garlic

Sea salt

2 ½ cups (625 mL) **carnaroli, arborio or vialone nano rice (we prefer Acquerello carnaroli)** (18 oz/500 g)

1 cup (250 mL) **white wine**

3 ½ oz (100 g) **finely grated fresh Parmesan** (1 cup/250 mL), **for finishing**

2 Tbsp (30 mL) **chopped Italian (flat-leaf) parsley, for finishing**

1 ½–2 Tbsp (22–30 mL) **unsalted butter, for finishing**

In a large pot, bring the saffron and stock to a boil. Remove from the heat, and set aside for 30 minutes to allow the saffron to infuse the stock. Immediately reheat the stock.

In a medium saucepan, heat the oil and butter over low heat until just starting to sizzle. Add the onion and garlic, and sweat until soft and translucent, about 15 minutes. Season with salt.

Add the rice, and sweat until it starts to "click" (see the tip on page 214), about 1 minute.

Add the wine and let it reduce completely, about 15 minutes.

Add the stock to the rice a ladle at a time, letting it reduce completely between each addition.

Cook until all of the stock has been used and the rice is slightly al dente. Remove from the heat and add the Parmesan, parsley and butter, combining thoroughly.

GREMOLATA

Zest of 6 lemons (use microplane)

3 cloves garlic, finely minced

½ cup (125 mL) **chopped Italian (flat-leaf) parsley**

Gently mix the ingredients together.

Best to use immediately, or store in the fridge for up to 1 day.

Slow-cooked crispy pork belly — grilled octopus, soft polenta and rapini — salsa verde

Brined and cooked pork belly *page 146*

14 oz (400 g) **octopus tentacles, raw or cooked**

¼ cup (60 mL) **Salsa Verde** *page 220*

2 large bunches rapini

4 Tbsp (60 mL) **canola oil, divided**

Olive oil, for dressing octopus

Sea salt and freshly ground black pepper

½ recipe Soft Polenta (do not shape or fry) *page 166* **or Polenta alla Griglia** *page 165*

2 Tbsp (30 mL) **extra virgin olive oil**

1 clove garlic

At least 2 days before you plan to serve this dish, brine the pork, and then cook the pork the next day.

On serving day or beforehand, cook the octopus if using raw (see the tip on page 144), and prepare the salsa verde (ideally the day before so that the flavours have time to blend).

Remove the cooked pork from the fridge. Trim any excess fat and cut into 4 portions.

Preheat the oven to 425°F (220°C). Light a wood-fired barbecue, or preheat a gas or charcoal grill or cast-iron grill pan.

Bring a pot of salted water to a boil. Have ready a large bowl full of ice water. Cook the rapini until just tender, 2 to 3 minutes, and plunge into the ice. Once it's cool, drain and pat dry.

Heat an ovenproof frying pan, and add 2 Tbsp (30 mL) of the canola oil. Put the pork belly into the pan, skin side down. As soon as the pork starts to sizzle, transfer the pan to the oven and cook until the skin is crispy and cracked, about 15 minutes.

Coat the octopus lightly in olive oil, season with salt and pepper and grill until you see grill marks. Diagonally slice the octopus into ¾-inch-thick (2 cm) pieces.

Prepare the polenta. For the soft polenta, follow only the first 2 steps of the recipe. (You'll be serving the polenta soft, and not setting in the fridge and frying it.)

In a large frying pan, heat the olive oil. Add the garlic and rapini and sauté lightly.

To serve, spread about 1 Tbsp (15 mL) salsa on 4 plates. Place a spoonful of the soft polenta on top, then a piece of the pork, crispy-skin side up. Drape a piece of octopus on top of the pork, and another piece beside it. Then place the rapini around and on top of the pork.

Continued overleaf

WINE NOTE Riesling always comes to mind for pork. Red wine pairings include some of Piedmont's finest: Barbera or Barolo.

COOKING RAW OCTOPUS

Clean the tentacles by placing in a stainless steel bowl and drizzling with olive oil and a generous amount of salt. Massage for 2 minutes. Let stand for 15 minutes, then rinse under cold running water and pat dry.

Fill a large pot with salted water and bring to a boil. Dip the octopus 3 times into the boiling water, for 3 seconds each time. Then place the octopus into the boiling water with the head facing upward and reduce the water to a gentle simmer. Add 1 large onion, peeled and sliced, and a bay leaf and cook for 1 hour.

Turn the octopus over so that it is head down and cook for another 30 minutes. Remove the octopus from the water and let cool at room temperature.

Cut the tentacles into 3-inch (8 cm) pieces.

BRINING THE PORK BELLY

5 lbs (2.3 kg) **pork belly**

5 quarts (5 L) **cold water**

1 ⅔ cups (410 mL) **Himalayan pink salt** (14 oz/400 g)

¾ cup (185 mL) **granulated sugar** (6 oz/170 g)

½ **leek, both white and green part**

½ **onion**

½ **carrot**

½ **head garlic, cut through horizontally (cloves kept together and unpeeled)**

2 sprigs **fresh thyme**

4 **fresh or dried bay leaves**

1 Tbsp (15 mL) **black peppercorns**

Rinse the pork belly to remove any blood. Using a blowtorch, gently burn off any hair with a low flame.

In a very large nonreactive container that will fit into your fridge, combine the water, salt, sugar, leek, onion, carrot, garlic, herbs and peppercorns. Whisk vigorously to dissolve the salt.

Submerge the pork belly in the brine, cover with a tight-fitting lid or plastic wrap and refrigerate for 24 hours.

The following day, remove the pork belly, rinse and pat dry.

COOKING THE PORK BELLY

1 **Bouquet Garni** *page 215*

1 large **carrot, peeled**

1 large **onion**

1 large **leek, white part only**

1 large **stalk celery**

1 **brined pork belly**

1 **head garlic, cut through horizontally (cloves kept together and unpeeled)**

Prepare the bouquet garni.

Preheat the oven to 325°F (160°C).

Roughly chop the vegetables. Put the pork in a large, heavy-bottomed pot with the vegetables, bouquet garni and garlic. Pour in enough water to cover the pork by 4 inches (10 cm). Bring to a boil, and then lower the heat to a gentle simmer. Cover with a cartouche (see the tip on page 97), then place a lid on the pot. Cook in the oven for 3 ½ hours, until the meat can be easily pierced with a knife and is almost falling apart.

Remove from the oven, and let rest for 2 hours. Discard the vegetables.

Prepare a baking sheet that is large enough to hold the meat by lining it with parchment paper. Place the meat on the baking sheet. Place another piece of parchment paper and a second sheet on top of the pork, and place a heavy weight on it to press the pork. Chill in the fridge until the pork becomes cold, preferably overnight.

PORK

In a world of giant grocery store chains and the huge farms and ranches that supply them, we've lost our direct relationship with the original goodness and flavours of our food. Fortunately, we are now seeing a trend to return to natural, original sources. This trend is perhaps nowhere more pronounced than in the worlds of poultry and pork.

Of those two, pork is the more profound revelation. If you have been existing solely on supermarket meat, you may find the flavour of organic, free-range hogs that have lived a happy, full life to be almost shocking. The pork available to us now is fantastic, full of flavour. It's almost like going back seventy-five years, nothing like supermarket product at all.

Pork is obviously very versatile. Without pork there would be no prosciutto, capicollo or salami. Nor Bolognese sauce. And you can use the cooking juices from roasting pork in sauces and other recipes.

CinCin's slow-roasted pork belly, served alongside grilled Pacific octopus, is a textbook example of how rich, vibrant and deep the flavour of great pork can be. Depending on the time of year, you might even find a chop on the menu. No matter what part of the animal is used, pork at CinCin rises to the level of delicacy. ——————————

CORNERSTONE
INGREDIENT

CONTORNI

Braised carrots

24 new-season carrots (preferably tri-colour)

2 Tbsp (30 mL) canola oil

¼ cup (60 mL) unsalted butter

Sea salt

1 Tbsp (15 mL) granulated sugar

2 sprigs fresh tarragon

2 fresh or dried bay leaves

6 white peppercorns

Chopped Italian (flat-leaf) parsley, for garnish

Wash the carrots but do not peel.

Heat the oil and butter in a large heavy sauté pan over moderate heat. When melted and sizzling, add the carrots and gently cook for 2 minutes, seasoning with salt as they cook.

After 2 minutes, add enough cold water to cover the carrots by 1 inch (2.5 cm). Add the sugar, tarragon, bay leaves and peppercorns. Bring to a boil, lower the heat to a gentle simmer and check the seasoning, adding more salt or sugar if necessary. Cook until carrots can be barely pierced with the tip of a sharp knife.

Remove from the heat, and allow the carrots to cool in the pan.

Remove the carrots from the cooking liquid and place in a clean pan. Add enough of the cooking liquid to come halfway up the carrots. Cook vigorously until the liquid has evaporated and the carrots are coated in the buttery sauce that's left in the pan.

Add some parsley and serve immediately.

Sautéed Swiss chard

SERVES 4

24 stalks Swiss or rainbow chard

3 Tbsp (45 mL) olive oil

1 clove garlic, finely minced

Sea salt

¾ cup (185 mL) White Chicken Stock *page 215*
or Vegetable Stock *page 217*

Separate the centre stems from the chard leaves. Chop the stems into 3-inch (8 cm) pieces, and cut each leaf into 4 equal pieces.

Bring a pot of salted water to a boil. Have ready a large bowl full of ice water. Cook the chard stems until just tender, about 5 minutes. Submerge in the ice water to cool, then drain and pat dry.

Heat a large sauté pan over moderate heat. Add the olive oil and garlic, and cook gently for 2 minutes, being careful not to brown.

Stir the leaves in quickly and season with salt. Add the stock, turn the heat up to high and bring to a boil. Cook vigorously for about a minute, stirring from time to time, until the leaves start to wilt.

Add the stems and continue cooking until the stock is completely reduced. Correct the seasoning.

Giant white beans

(Gigante Beans)

1 ¼ cups (310 mL) **dried white gigante (or cannellini) beans** (9 oz/250 g)

2 Tbsp (30 mL) **baking soda**

1 large tomato

½ head garlic, cut through horizontally (cloves kept together and unpeeled)

1 carrot, peeled and left whole

1 leek, white part only, left whole

1 onion, peeled and left whole

1 stalk celery

1 Bouquet Garni *page 215*

Sea salt and freshly ground black pepper

The night before serving, soak the beans with the baking soda and enough cold water to cover them by 2 inches (5 cm). Leave at room temperature overnight.

The following day, drain and rinse the beans under cold, running water. Place in a pot and cover with fresh cold water, again covering by 2 inches (5 cm). Add all of the remaining ingredients. Bring to a boil, then lower the heat to a gentle simmer. Remove any scum as it forms on the surface. Cook until tender and creamy, about 2 hours.

When the beans have cooled, remove the vegetables from the cooking liquid, and season the beans with salt and pepper. Store in the cooking liquid until ready to serve.

You can serve this in a ramekin in the middle of the table for everyone to share, along with bread, crostini and olives.

Chickpea purée
(Hummus)

5 cloves Whole Roasted Garlic *page 163*

One 28 oz (796 mL) **can chickpeas**
(or 3 cups/750 mL cooked)

6 Tbsp (90 mL) **crème fraîche**

¼ cup (60 mL) **fresh lemon juice**

3 Tbsp (45 mL) **tahini (sesame paste)**

1 cup (250 mL) **olive oil**

Sea salt and freshly ground black pepper

Prepare the roasted garlic if you don't have any on hand.

In a blender or food processor, combine the chickpeas, roasted garlic, crème fraîche, lemon juice and tahini. Slowly pour in the olive oil, and blend until smooth and well combined.

Pass the hummus through a *tamis* (also known as a drum sieve, which is a flat sieve in the shape of a drum or cake pan) using a food scraper or spatula, or use a regular fine-meshed sieve. This will give the hummus a velvety texture. Season to taste with salt and pepper.

Best served warm.

This works well with grilled fish and meat.
It's also delicious on toasted or grilled bread.

Fennel-onion confit

1 **Bouquet Garni** *page 215*

6 medium bulbs **fennel**

3 medium **yellow onions**

¾ **cup** (185 mL) **water**

½ **lb** (220 g) **unsalted butter** (1 cup/250 mL)

1 **Tbsp** (15 mL) **sea salt**

Freshly ground black pepper

Prepare the bouquet garni.

Trim the base of the fennel, and remove the stalks and the outer layer. Cut the fennel in half, cutting through the top to the base so that you have 2 wide halves. Remove the core.

Lay the halves cut side down on a chopping board, and slice with the grain into ¼-inch (6 mm) strips. Reserve in a large bowl.

Repeat the process with the onion. Add the slices to the fennel.

In a large ovenproof sauté pan, heat the water. Whisk in the butter 2 Tbsp (30 mL) at a time, making sure the water does not boil. When all of the butter has been incorporated, add the fennel, onion and salt.

Stir together—or use your hands to massage the mixture together, making sure the fennel and onion are coated with the salt, butter and water.

Add the bouquet garni, cover with a cartouche (see the tip on page 95) and cook slowly, stirring occasionally, for up to 2 hours, or until the fennel and onion are very soft. Add more water if the mixture becomes dry. Check and correct the seasoning with salt and pepper.

Keep in a sealed container in the fridge for 5 to 6 days.

Eggplant Parmigiana

2 large globe eggplant

Sea salt

About ¾ cup (185 mL) olive oil, divided

1 small onion, minced

1 clove garlic, crushed with back of knife

2 cups (500 mL) canned peeled Roma tomatoes (with juice)

Freshly ground black pepper

½ lb (220 g) buffalo mozzarella or bocconcini, cut into ¼-inch (6 mm) slices

1 bunch fresh basil, torn

3 ½ oz (100 g) freshly grated Parmesan (1 cup/250 mL)

Chopped Italian (flat-leaf) parsley, for garnish

Cut the eggplant into ¼-inch-thick (6 mm) rounds. Salt the slices, lay them in a colander, rinse them and let them sit for 30 minutes.

Meanwhile, heat 2 Tbsp (30 mL) of the olive oil in a medium frying pan, and cook the onion and garlic until soft, being careful not to brown. Season with a pinch of salt.

Add the tomatoes, stirring frequently to break them up. Cook until the tomatoes start to stick to the bottom of the pan.

Press the sauce through a fine-meshed sieve or pass through a food mill. Discard the pulp, and season the sauce to taste with salt and pepper.

Pat the eggplant dry. Heat 2 Tbsp (30 mL) of the olive oil in a large frying pan, and cook a single layer of the eggplant until the slices are slightly coloured on both sides. Set aside on paper towels. Continue cooking in batches, using more olive oil for each batch.

Preheat the oven to 375°F (190°C).

Lightly oil 4 small earthenware ovenproof dishes. (Ours are 6 ½ inches/17 cm square and 1 inch/2.5 cm deep.)

To assemble, spoon some tomato sauce in the bottom of each dish. Add a single layer of cooked eggplant, then the mozzarella, then some basil leaves and finally a sprinkling of Parmesan. Repeat these layers once more, then finish with an additional layer of eggplant and more Parmesan.

Bake until the surface starts to bubble, about 20 to 25 minutes.

Serve straight from the oven, sprinkled with the chopped parsley.

Pancetta comes in two types: flat and rolled. You want the flat kind for this recipe. Instead of buying it presliced at the deli, you can cut it into paper-thin slices yourself by putting it in the freezer first. Or you can dice the pancetta instead. Peeled, precooked chestnuts should be easy to find at Italian delis.

Brussels sprouts — chestnuts, pancetta, parsley

SERVES 4

1 ¼ lbs (570 g) **Brussels sprouts**

4 oz (110 g) **whole piece flat pancetta (or buy it sliced)**

2 Tbsp (30 mL) **unsalted butter**

Sea salt

About 4 cups (1 L) **White Chicken Stock**
page 215

3 Tbsp (45 mL) **cooked and peeled chestnuts** (1 ½ oz/40 g)

2 Tbsp (30 mL) **chopped Italian (flat-leaf) parsley**

Remove the outer leaves from the Brussels sprouts. Using a sharp knife, cut a ¼-inch (6 mm) cross into the base of each sprout.

Preheat the oven to 450°F (230°C). Line an 11 × 17-inch (28 × 43 cm) baking sheet with parchment paper.

Cut the pancetta into paper-thin slices. Put onto the baking sheet in a single layer, and cook in the oven until golden brown, about 5 minutes. Remove from the oven and bring to room temperature. Crumble into pieces. Alternatively, cut the pancetta into ½-inch (1 cm) dice, and fry until golden brown, 2 to 3 minutes. Let it cool on paper towels.

Heat the butter in a large sauté pan over moderate heat until it starts to sizzle. Add the Brussels sprouts, and toss in the butter. Cook for 2 to 3 minutes, seasoning with salt as they cook.

Add the stock, making sure there's enough to completely cover the sprouts. Bring to a boil and cook vigorously until the stock has reduced by half.

Add the chestnuts, and continue cooking until the stock has reduced to almost nothing and the sprouts are coated in the butter.

Add the parsley and mix thoroughly.

To serve, pour into a serving dish and scatter with the pancetta.

At CinCin, we divide the onion/garlic mixture between four sauté pans and sauté each of the other vegetables with them separately, with a sprig of thyme, to cook them to perfection. But you can also cook everything together, as written in the recipe.

Giambotta

Pictured on page 13

SERVES 4

3 large globe eggplant

3 zucchini

1 red bell pepper

1 yellow bell pepper

1 Roma tomato

1 onion

2 cloves garlic

1 ¼ cups (310 mL) **extra virgin olive oil, divided**

4 sprigs fresh thyme

Sea salt and freshly ground black pepper

Fresh basil leaves, torn, for garnish (optional)

GRILLING BREAD

Slices of grilled rustic loaf go very well with the giambotta. At CinCin we make our own bread, but a lot of stores carry very good sourdough. Ciabatta is perfect. Cut the bread into ½-inch (1 cm) slices, dress them with a little olive oil and grill on a barbecue or in a cast-iron grill pan. When the bread is nicely marked, remove it from the grill and rub with a clove of garlic and season with a pinch of salt.

Dice the eggplant, zucchini, peppers and tomato in ½-inch (1 cm) pieces.

Mince the onion and garlic.

Heat ½ cup (125 mL) of the olive oil in a medium sauté pan, add the onion and garlic and cook for 10 minutes. (You'll be putting them in the pan first, as they need to cook slowly until very tender; bringing out the full and natural sweetness of both the onions and garlic is very important.)

Add the bell peppers and thyme, along with ¼ cup (60 mL) more oil, and cook for 15 minutes.

Add the zucchini and ¼ cup (60 mL) more oil, and cook for 8 to 10 minutes.

Add the eggplant and ¼ cup (60 mL) more oil, and cook for about 5 minutes.

As the vegetables cook, season gently with salt and pepper. When the vegetables are totally soft but still holding their shape, cool them slightly and remove the thyme.

Return to a gentle heat and stir in the tomatoes. Check the seasoning. You can also stir in a small quantity of torn basil at the last moment.

Garlic, rosemary and sea salt roast potatoes

2 ¼ lbs (1 kg) new-season potatoes (preferably Sieglinde/German butter), unpeeled

2 heads garlic, cloves peeled and left whole

2 sprigs fresh thyme

2 sprigs Italian (flat-leaf) parsley

4 sprigs fresh rosemary, divided

Sea salt

¼ cup (60 mL) extra virgin olive oil

Place the whole potatoes, garlic, thyme, parsley, 2 sprigs of the rosemary and salt in a heavy-bottomed saucepan, and cover with cold water by 2 inches (5 cm). Bring to a boil, lower the heat to a gentle simmer and cook until the potatoes are just tender. Turn the heat off, and allow to cool completely in the pan.

Preheat the oven to 450°F (230°C).

Drain the potatoes. Discard the herbs and cut the garlic into uneven chunks.

Heat the olive oil in a large heavy ovenproof pan. Add the potatoes, garlic and remaining rosemary, and sauté gently for 5 minutes to give colour and flavour. Season with a good pinch of sea salt.

Roast in the oven for about 10 to 12 minutes, until the skins are crisp.

Garlic is a health food and flavour enhancer in one potent package. Garlic has an umami effect. If you use it carefully, it adds so much flavour without making the food taste "garlicky."

With its proven ability to improve many health problems, this close relative of the onion has served as a medicine and food supplement since as early as 7000 BC. A Mediterranean staple for thousands of years, garlic was first used in Asia. Today, China grows 80 percent of the world's annual twenty-five-million-ton production.

During the year we buy a lot of garlic—including red Russian, music and elephant garlic—from Gabriel at Sapo Bravo Organics, just northwest of Lytton. We use it in so many ways. Just browse through the cookbook and you will see: whole heads, chips, stocks and sauces, purées—garlic is invaluable. ——————————

CORNERSTONE
INGREDIENT

Whole roasted garlic

(Garlic Confit)

6 heads garlic

About 4 cups (1 L) **extra virgin olive oil, to cover garlic**

2 sprigs fresh rosemary

2 sprigs fresh thyme

Preheat the oven to 250°F (120°C).

Clean the garlic of any loose skin or dirt. Trim the root hairs, and place the heads in a medium-sized heavy ovenproof sauté pan or saucepan. Cover with the olive oil, and add the rosemary and thyme. Place the pan over gentle heat, and warm until the oil just starts to bubble.

Cover and place in the oven for at least 2 hours, or until you can easily squash the garlic between 2 fingers. Cool to room temperature.

You can remove the garlic from the oil to use immediately, or leave the garlic in the oil and store in a sealed container in the fridge for up to 1 month. To serve from the fridge, simply bring to room temperature and remove from the oil.

Gnocchi Romani

4 cups (1 L) **whole milk**

2 cups (500 mL) **semolina flour** (7 oz/200 g)

3 egg yolks

4 ½ oz (125 g) **freshly grated Parmesan**
(1 ¼ cups/310 mL)

5 ¼ oz (150 g) **unsalted butter** (½ cup + 3 Tbsp/
170 mL)

Freshly grated nutmeg

Sea salt and freshly ground black pepper

1 ½ Tbsp (22 mL) **unsalted butter, softened,
for baking the gnocchi**

**Freshly grated Parmesan, for baking the
gnocchi**

Lightly grease a 10-inch (25 cm) pie plate or nonstick sauté pan with canola oil.

Bring the milk to a boil in a large heavy-bottomed pot.

Lower the heat and slowly whisk in the semolina flour. Cook the mixture for 15 minutes, stirring frequently. Remove from the heat, and cool for 5 minutes.

Work in the egg yolks one at a time until completely combined.

Add the Parmesan, as well as the 5 ¼ oz (150 g) butter about 1 ½ Tbsp (22 mL) at a time, and work vigorously until fully combined. Season with nutmeg and salt and pepper.

Spread the mixture evenly to a 1 ¼-inch (3 cm) thickness on the prepared pie plate or sauté pan. Cover the top with parchment and another pie plate or pan. Place a light weight on top to compress. Cool in the fridge until completely set, up to 3 hours.

Cut and shape into eight 2 ½-inch-long (6 cm) cylinders that are 1 ¼ inches (3 cm) thick, and place in a small baguette pan (we use Matfer 60). Or cut into 8 wedges. Place the gnocchi back in the fridge for about 1 hour to firm up.

Preheat the oven to 400°F (200°C). Line an 11 × 17-inch (28 × 43 cm) baking sheet with parchment paper, and lightly grease the parchment with oil. (If you're baking only half the gnocchi, use a 9 × 13-inch/ 23 × 33 cm baking sheet, and store the rest in a covered container in the fridge. It will keep for 4 to 5 days.)

Place the gnocchi on the parchment with some space in between. Dot each gnocchi with 1 tsp (5 mL) of butter, and lightly cover it with Parmesan. Bake for 8 minutes until golden brown and slightly puffy. Serve immediately.

Polenta alla griglia

(Grilled Polenta)

7 cups (1.75 L) **water**

Sea salt

2 cups (500 mL) **polenta meal or coarsely ground yellow cornmeal** (12¼ oz/350 g), **plus more for dusting**

5¼ oz (150 g) **unsalted butter** (½ cup + 3 Tbsp/ 170 mL), **softened**

7 oz (200 g) **freshly grated Parmesan** (2 cups/500 mL)

Freshly ground black pepper

In a large saucepan, boil the water with a good pinch of salt.

Lower the heat to a gentle simmer, and whisk in the polenta or cornmeal in a slow, steady stream. Cook for 40 minutes on a gentle heat, stirring frequently.

Remove from the heat, and add the butter and Parmesan, stirring vigorously to fully incorporate. Correct the seasoning with salt and pepper.

Line an 11 × 17-inch (28 × 43 cm) baking sheet with parchment. Spread the polenta onto the baking sheet at least ½ inch (1 cm) thick. At the restaurant, we allow it to set unevenly (imagine a small mountain range!). Cool completely overnight in the fridge uncovered.

Cut the polenta into fifteen 2-inch-wide (5 cm) pieces (2 per person). Each piece should be about 3 oz (85 g) each.

Light a wood-fired barbecue, or preheat a gas or charcoal grill or cast-iron grill pan.

Dust the polenta pieces in cornmeal and grill until nicely coloured and warmed to the centre.

Cornmeal is a staple of Italian cooking, and it's prepared in a variety of ways as an accompaniment to many dishes. This recipe showcases two preparations: soft polenta, which we serve with our Slow-Cooked Crispy Pork Belly (page 143), and sautéed polenta, which we serve with our Duck with Richmond Corn Cooked in Embers (page 120).

Polenta, two ways

(Soft and Sautéed)

3 cups (750 mL) **whole milk**

3 cups (750 mL) **water**

1 ¾ cups (435 mL) **instant polenta meal or finely ground yellow cornmeal** (9 oz/250 g)

5 ¼ oz (150 g) **unsalted butter** (½ cup + 3 Tbsp/ 170 mL), **softened**

7 oz (200 g) **freshly grated Parmesan** (1 cup/250 mL)

Sea salt and freshly ground black pepper

Neutral oil (canola, sunflower, grapeseed), for frying polenta

To make the soft polenta, follow the first two steps of this recipe. Complete the remaining steps to make the set and sautéed version.

Combine the milk and water in a heavy-bottomed pot and bring to a boil. Lower the heat to a gentle simmer, and whisk in the flour in a slow, constant stream. Using a spoon, vigorously beat the polenta mixture for 2 minutes.

Remove from the heat. Add the butter in 1-inch (2.5 cm) pieces and the Parmesan, mixing vigorously to combine. Season with salt and pepper.

Line an 11 × 17-inch (28 × 43 cm) rimmed baking sheet with parchment. Spread the polenta onto the parchment at least 1 inch (2.5 cm) thick. Cover with parchment and another baking sheet, and press with a light weight. Allow to cool and completely set, up to 3 hours.

Preheat the oven to 425°F (220°C).

Cut the polenta into fifteen 2 ½-inch-wide (6 cm) pieces (2 per person). Each piece should be about 3 oz (85 g) each.

Heat a thin film of the oil in a medium ovenproof nonstick frying pan. When the pan is hot, add polenta (no more than 4 pieces in a 10-inch/25 cm pan) and cook until the edges start to caramelize, about 1 minute.

Move the pan to the oven and bake for 5 minutes.

Flip the polenta and return to the oven for a further 5 minutes.

Remove from the oven, drain on paper towels and serve.

Rosemary and Parmesan focaccia with olive oil and tapenade

1 cup (250 mL) **Bread Starter** *overleaf*

1 ¾ cups (435 mL) **warm water** (90°F/32°C)

¼ cup (60 mL) **olive oil**

1 tsp (5 mL) **active dry yeast**

5 ½ cups (1375 mL) **bread flour** (1½ lbs/670 g)

1 Tbsp (15 mL) **salt**

2 tsp (10 mL) **chopped fresh rosemary**

2 tsp (10 mL) **dried oregano**

Freshly grated Parmesan, coarse sea salt and extra virgin olive oil, for baking the focaccia

Green Olive and Garlic Confit Tapenade *overleaf*

Two 16 × 12 × 2-inch (40 × 30 × 5 cm) **pans or four 9 × 5-inch** (23 × 12 cm) **loaf pans** (or one 11 × 17-inch/28 × 43 cm baking sheet)

OPTIONAL BAKING METHOD

If you don't have a baking sheet or another baking pan that fits inside the first baking pan to keep the bread flat as it bakes, use this method instead. After proofing the bread the first time, use your fingers to push holes in the focaccia to form small wells. Add the cheese and some more chopped rosemary, and drizzle with the olive oil. Continue with the second proofing. Bake at the same temperature, turning the bread 180 degrees at the 10-minute mark and baking for a further 10 minutes.

On the day before, prepare the bread starter, as it needs 24 hours in the fridge before you can bake with it.

Lightly grease one 16 × 12 × 2-inch (40 × 30 × 5 cm) pan, or two 9 × 5-inch (23 × 12 cm) loaf pans. You'll need another pan the same size to fit inside the pan(s) with the dough. (If you don't have this, you can use an 11 × 17-inch/28 × 43 cm baking sheet; see the tip below for baking instructions.)

In a small bowl or measuring cup, whisk together the water, oil and yeast, and set aside.

Combine the flour, salt, herbs and bread starter in a mixing bowl or the bowl of a stand mixer fitted with a dough hook attachment.

Add the yeast mixture, and knead, either on medium speed in the stand mixer for 15 minutes or by hand for 15 to 20 minutes, until the dough feels elastic and is very smooth.

Place the dough on a clean work surface, and roll into a rectangle around 2 inches (5 cm) thick.

Place the dough in the prepared pan; it will be about half the size of the pan. Cover with a damp cloth, and allow to proof in a warm place for about 1 hour, or until doubled in size.

Very lightly oil the proofed dough, and stretch to the size of the pan, all the way into the corners.

Sprinkle Parmesan evenly over the top, and proof in a warm place for about 30 minutes, or until doubled again in size.

Meanwhile, prepare the tapenade.

Toward the end of this second proofing, preheat the oven to 400°F (200°C).

Sprinkle the proofed loaf lightly with coarse sea salt, cover with 1 sheet of parchment paper and another baking pan or heavy baking sheet that's the same size.

Bake for 10 minutes. Remove the second tray and parchment paper, and bake for 10 more minutes for a total of 20 minutes' baking time. Brush with more olive oil when it comes out of the oven.

Serve warm with the tapenade, butter, or olive oil and balsamic vinegar.

BREAD STARTER

½ tsp (2.5 mL) **active dry yeast**

½ cup (125 mL) **warm water** (90°F/32°C)

1 ¾ cups + 2 Tbsp (465 mL) **all-purpose flour** (½ lb/220 g)

In a measuring cup or small bowl, mix the yeast into the water until dissolved.

Place the flour in a large mixing bowl, and pour in the water and yeast. Mix well with your hands. The mixture should be slightly wet and lump free.

Place in a large sealed container at least 3 times the size of the starter, as it will double in size overnight. Store in the fridge for at least 24 hours before using, or up to 4 days.

GREEN OLIVE AND GARLIC CONFIT TAPENADE

1 small head **garlic**

1 cup (250 mL) **extra virgin olive oil**

2 cups (500 mL) **pimento-stuffed green olives**

1 small bunch **Italian (flat-leaf) parsley,** chopped

Separate and peel the garlic cloves and leave them whole. Place in a small saucepan with the olive oil, and cook over low heat until soft, about 10 minutes. Set aside to cool.

Drain the olives from the brine and rinse well.

In a food processor or blender, combine the olives, parsley and the cooled garlic and olive oil, and blend to a coarse texture. Adjust the consistency by adding more olive oil, if desired.

Keeps in a sealed container in the fridge for 1 week.

DOLCI

Warm dark chocolate fondant — Caramélia gelato and fresh berries

Caramélia Gelato *overleaf*

5 ½ oz (160 g) **70 % dark chocolate**

5 ¼ oz (150 g) **unsalted butter** (½ cup + 3 Tbsp/ 170 mL)

5 eggs

¾ cup (185 mL) **granulated sugar**

¼ cup (60 mL) **bread flour, sifted**

Fresh berries, for garnish

Equipment: Nine 2 ½-inch (6 cm) **metal rings** (1 extra fondant to test cooking time)

Start the gelato at least a day before serving so that it can chill overnight in the fridge before you churn it.

For the fondant, in a small saucepan on the stove or in a bowl in the microwave, melt the chocolate and the butter together to 122°F (50°C) and set aside.

Place the eggs and sugar in the bowl of a stand mixer fitted with a whisk attachment, and whisk on high speed for at least 10 minutes, until doubled in size.

Fold in the melted chocolate and butter with a rubber spatula.

Fold in the flour.

Place in a piping bag, and let set in the fridge for 2 hours. (You can also use a metal bowl instead of a piping bag.)

Line nine 2 ½-inch (6 cm) metal rings with strips of parchment paper, and spray with canola oil. (You can also use small ramekins instead of the metal rings.)

To cook the fondant, preheat the oven to 375°F (190°C). Have ready a small baking sheet, and a large one that will fit 8 of the metal rings. Cut out 9 square pieces of parchment paper that are larger than the metal ring.

Place a piece of parchment and a lined metal ring on your scale. Note the weight. Pipe (or use an ice cream scoop) to fill the metal ring with 2 ½ oz (70 g) of the fondant. Make sure not to leave any air pockets. Carefully transfer to the large baking sheet. Repeat with the rest of the metal rings, transferring the last one to the small baking sheet.

It's a good idea to first cook one separately to find out the exact cooking time for your oven. Take it out after 10 minutes. The fondant should be runny in the middle. Carefully remove the metal ring, unwrap the parchment and transfer it to a plate; it should not crack or break. If it does begin to crack as you move it, increase the cooking time by 1 minute.

Serve with the freshest berries and 1 scoop of gelato.

Continued overleaf

1 lb (450 g) **Valrhona Caramélia chocolate (or other caramel-flavoured milk chocolate), divided**

5 cups (1.25 L) **whole milk**

2 Tbsp (30 mL) **milk powder**

⅓ cup (80 mL) **granulated sugar**

½ cup (125 mL) **glucose powder**

see tip on page 185

Divide the chocolate into 2 portions, 11 oz (310 g) and 5 oz (140 g).

Place the milk in a large saucepan over medium-high heat.

When the temperature reaches 77°F (25°C), whisk in the milk powder.

At 85°F (30°C), mix in the sugar and glucose powder. Continue mixing and heating.

At 105°F (40°C), add the 11 oz (310 g) of chocolate. Whisk until the gelato reaches 185°F (85°C). All of the chocolate should be melted and the mixture should be nice and smooth.

Remove from the heat, and pass through a fine-meshed sieve into a large bowl, and chill in the fridge overnight.

The next day, place a large metal bowl in the freezer to chill.

Chop the remaining 5 oz (140 g) of chocolate and set aside.

Churn the chilled gelato in an ice cream machine according to the manufacturer's instructions.

Place the churned gelato in the chilled bowl from the freezer and combine with the chopped chocolate, mixing well.

Keeps in the freezer in a tightly sealed container for up to 1 week.

Start this recipe one or two days ahead. First make the crema (which goes inside the mousse), as it needs four hours to freeze. The sponge cake and the glaze can be made in the meantime. (Store the glaze in the fridge to be reheated at serving time.) You can make the mousse on serving day, but it will need at least four hours in the freezer to come out of the square mold nicely.

Chocolate mousse

MAKES 20

Chocolate Crema *overleaf*

Chocolate Sponge Cake *overleaf*

Dark Chocolate Glaze *overleaf*

4 egg yolks

3 Tbsp (45 mL) **granulated sugar**

1 lb (450 g) **40% milk chocolate**
(or 3 cups/750 mL chips)

¾ cup (185 mL) **whole milk**

¾ cup (185 mL) **heavy cream**

2 cups (500 mL) **softly whipped cream**

Equipment: Twenty 2-inch (5 cm) **silicone dome molds or ice-cube trays**

Twenty 3-inch (8 cm) **square molds or square rings**

This dessert will require at least twenty 2-inch (5 cm) dome-shaped silicone molds (or silicone ice-cube trays) for the crema, and twenty 3-inch (8 cm) molds or square rings that are about 3 inches (8 cm) high to accommodate the cake base, crema, and mousse.

At least 1 day before serving day, make the crema.

While it freezes, make the sponge cake and the chocolate glaze.

Take the 3-inch (8 cm) square molds or square rings and place them on a baking sheet. Put a piece of cake at the bottom of the mold. Unmold the crema and place it on top of the cake. Store in the freezer until ready to be filled with the mousse.

To make the mousse, in a medium bowl, whisk together the yolks and sugar.

If the chocolate is a solid block, chop into small pieces. Place the pieces or chips in a medium bowl and set aside.

In a small saucepan, bring the milk and cream to a boil over medium-high heat. Pour half the mixture into the yolks and sugar very slowly while whisking, to avoid scrambling the eggs.

Whisk well, and add the whole bowl to the remaining cream and milk in the saucepan.

Stirring with a silicone rubber spatula over medium-low heat, cook the anglaise until it thickens and reaches 185°F (85°C).

Immediately strain this hot mixture through a fine-meshed sieve into the bowl of chocolate to melt it, and combine well, finishing with an immersion blender to get rid of any lumps and air bubbles. Cool the mixture to 95°F (35°C).

Fold in the whipped cream. *Continued overleaf*

Carefully fill the molds that contain the cake and crema with the mousse all the way to the top, smoothing over with a palette knife. Allow to freeze for at least 4 hours.

Remove the molds from the freezer. Using a blowtorch, carefully heat the sides of the square molds to release the mousses and place them on a wire rack.

If the glaze is in the fridge, warm it in the microwave until it reaches 95°F (35°C). If it is overheated, cool to that temperature. Hand blend or mix to remove any air bubbles.

Pour the glaze evenly over each mousse, making sure to get every corner and side.

Using a small palette knife, remove the mousses from the wire rack and place on a serving plate. Allow to fully defrost for 30 minutes before serving.

CHOCOLATE CREMA

6 egg yolks

¼ cup (60 mL) **granulated sugar**

½ lb (220 g) **70% dark chocolate** (or 1 ¹/₃ cups/330 mL chips)

1 cup (250 mL) **whole milk**

1 cup (250 mL) **heavy cream**

In a medium bowl, whisk together the yolks and sugar, and set aside.

If the chocolate is a solid block, chop into small pieces. Place the pieces or chips in a medium bowl and set aside.

In a small saucepan, bring the milk and cream to a boil over medium-high heat. Pour half the mixture into the yolks and sugar very slowly while whisking, to avoid scrambling the eggs. Whisk well, and add the whole bowl to the remaining cream and milk in the saucepan.

Stirring with a silicone rubber spatula over medium-low heat, cook the anglaise until it thickens and reaches 185°F (85°C).

Strain though a fine-meshed sieve into the bowl of chocolate and mix well to melt the chocolate, finishing with an immersion blender to get rid of any lumps and air bubbles.

Set out either your 2-inch (5 cm) silicone dome molds or ice-cube trays. Fill the molds to the top with the crema, and place in the freezer to freeze completely (at least 4 hours).

6 egg yolks

½ cup (125 mL) **granulated sugar**

¼ cup (60 mL) **all-purpose flour**

3 Tbsp (45 mL) **cornstarch**

3 Tbsp (45 mL) **cocoa powder (regular or Dutch process; we prefer Valrhona)**

3 Tbsp (45 mL) **unsalted butter**

4 egg whites

Preheat the oven to 350°F (180°C). Line two 11 × 17-inch (28 × 43 cm) baking sheets with parchment paper.

Place the egg yolks and sugar in the bowl of a stand mixer fitted with a whisk attachment, and turn on to medium speed. Continue mixing while you prepare the rest of the ingredients. It will need at least 10 minutes.

In a small bowl, sift together the flour, cornstarch and cocoa powder and set aside.

Melt the butter and set aside.

In another bowl, using a whisk or a hand mixer, whisk the egg whites until stiff and set aside.

Once the yolks and sugar have doubled in volume, remove the bowl and fold in the sifted dry ingredients using a spatula, combining thoroughly.

Add the butter and continue to fold.

Lastly, fold in the stiff egg whites, to lighten the mixture.

Spread the mixture evenly to cover the baking sheet. Bake in the oven for 10 minutes, or until slightly risen and a toothpick comes out clean. Set aside to cool.

Using 2-inch (5 cm) square cookie cutters or a knife, cut the cooled sponge cake into 2-inch (5 cm) squares.

DARK CHOCOLATE GLAZE

½ lb (220 g) **70% dark chocolate** (or 1 ¹/₃ cups/330 mL chips)

¾ cup (185 mL) **heavy cream**

If the chocolate is a solid block, chop into small pieces. Place the chocolate in a medium bowl.

In a medium saucepan, bring the cream to a boil. Immediately pour over the chocolate to melt it, finishing with an immersion blender to get rid of any lumps and air bubbles.

Can be stored in the fridge until ready to serve.

You will need a PolyScience Smoking Gun to smoke the milk for the gelato. Start this the day before, as the gelato needs to be chilled overnight before churning, and the brioche dough needs twenty-four hours to rise in the fridge. You can also use a brioche that you've previously made and frozen. Toast the brioche squares right before serving, or keep them in a sealed container until ready to use.

Maple-roasted apples — smoked-milk gelato, vanilla crumble and toasted brioche

SERVES 6

Brioche *overleaf*

Smoked-Milk Gelato *overleaf*

Brown Sugar and Vanilla Crumble *overleaf*

Toffee Sauce *overleaf*

6 apples (we prefer Gala and Pink Lady)

½ cup (125 mL) **maple syrup**

4 oz (110 g) **unsalted butter** (½ cup/125 mL)

1 vanilla bean

2 Tbsp (30 mL) **unsalted butter**

Kosher salt, for the brioche squares

3 to 5 amaranth or baby beet leaves, for garnish

At least a day before serving, start the brioche and the gelato. The next day, bake the brioche and churn the gelato.

Prepare the vanilla crumble and toffee sauce (both can also be prepared beforehand).

To roast the apples, preheat the oven to 350°F (180°C).

Peel and quarter the apples and cut out the cores. Cut each quarter in half, leaving you with 8 pieces per apple.

In a heavy ovenproof pan (cast iron is best), combine the maple syrup and butter. Scrape in the seeds of the vanilla bean (see the tip on page 208), and bring to a boil.

Add the apples and mix well. Once the apples are well coated, place the pan in the oven for about 15 minutes, or until the apples are fully cooked but not falling apart. Set aside at room temperature.

To toast brioche squares, preheat the oven to 325°F (160°C).

Use a bread knife to cut the brioche into 1-inch (2.5 cm) squares, and spread them on a baking sheet.

Melt the butter with a small pinch of salt, pour over the brioche squares and toss to coat.

Bake until crisp for 6 to 8 minutes, or until golden brown on all sides, turning every 3 minutes for even colour.

Reheat the toffee sauce in 30-second increments in the microwave until warm.

Place 6 to 8 pieces of apple on each plate with a few of the brioche squares. Add a spoonful of the crumble in the middle and the toffee sauce around the apples. Place a scoop of the smoked-milk gelato on top of the crumble and garnish with amaranth or beet leaves.

Continued overleaf

1 ¼ lbs (570 g) **unsalted butter**
(2 ½ cups/625 mL), **softened**

2 Tbsp (30 mL) **active dry yeast**

⅓ cup (80 mL) **whole milk**

14 eggs

10 cups (2.5 L) **all-purpose flour**
(2 lbs 10 oz/1.2 kg)

¾ cup (185 mL) **granulated sugar**

4 tsp (20 mL) **kosher salt**

Cut the butter into 1-inch (2.5 cm) pieces, and set aside.

Whisk together the yeast, milk and eggs in a large measuring jug and set aside.

Place the flour, sugar and salt into the bowl of a stand mixer fitted with a dough hook, and put it on a low speed. Add the milk/egg mixture and turn it up to medium speed.

Once a dough has formed (about 15 minutes), add the butter one piece at a time, allowing it to combine before adding the next piece of butter.

Oil a bowl that's big enough for your dough to at least double in size. Transfer the dough to the bowl, cover the top tightly with plastic wrap and place in the fridge for 24 hours.

After 24 hours, the dough will have risen and firmed up and will be ready to shape.

Cut the dough into 4 even pieces, and shape into four 4 × 12-inch (10 × 30 cm) loaf pans. Cover loosely with a tea towel. Leave in a warm, slightly humid area (such as on top of an oven) until doubled in size.

Preheat the oven to 400°F (200°C).

Bake the loaves for 20 minutes, then reduce the heat to 350°F (180°C) and bake for another 15 to 20 minutes.

Remove the brioche from the pans and cool on a wire rack.

These will keep very well in the freezer, fully wrapped, for up to a month. (Note that cutting the brioche for the toasted squares is easier when the bread is frozen.)

SMOKED-MILK GELATO

2 cups (500 mL) **whole milk**

¾ cup (185 mL) **heavy cream**

¾ cup (185 mL) **granulated sugar**

2 Tbsp (30 mL) **liquid glucose**
see tip on page 210

Equipment: PolyScience Smoking Gun

Pour the milk and cream into a deep bowl, and cover tightly with plastic wrap. Have ready some extra plastic wrap. Poke a small hole in the top, and insert the tube of the PolyScience Smoking Gun. Using a lighter, burn the smoking chips in the gun while the gun is on. You should start to see smoke filling the bowl. Smoke for 5 minutes. When the bowl is full of smoke, quickly remove the tube from the hole and cover the hole with more plastic wrap. Remove the wrap once the smoke has dissipated, after about 1 hour. (You can smoke the milk a second time if the flavour is not yet smoky enough.)

Place the smoked milk in a medium saucepan over medium heat. Whisk in the sugar and liquid glucose, and bring to a boil.

Turn off the heat and cool to room temperature. Place in the fridge to chill overnight.

Churn in an ice cream machine according to the manufacturer's instructions.

Keeps for up to 1 week in the freezer in a tightly sealed container.

BROWN SUGAR AND VANILLA CRUMBLE

¾ cup (185 mL) **packed brown sugar**

¼ cup (60 mL) **granulated sugar**

1 ¾ cups (435 mL) **all-purpose flour**

1 tsp (5 mL) **kosher salt**

1 **vanilla bean**

5 ¼ oz (150 g) **cold unsalted butter** (½ cup + 3 Tbsp/170 mL), **cut into cubes**

Preheat the oven to 325°F (160°C). Line an 11 × 17-inch (28 × 43 cm) baking sheet with parchment paper.

In a medium bowl, combine the sugars, flour and salt. Scrape in the seeds from the vanilla bean (see the tip on page 208).

Rub in the butter with your hands until the mixture resembles coarse bread crumbs.

Spread onto the prepared baking sheet, and bake for 4 minutes.

Mix well with a wooden spoon and return to the oven for another 4 minutes.

Repeat twice more, for a total baking time of 16 minutes.

Cool to room temperature. Can be kept in a sealed container for up to 3 days.

TOFFEE SAUCE

1 cup (250 mL) **packed brown sugar**

5 ¼ oz (150 g) **unsalted butter** (½ cup + 3 Tbsp/170 mL)

¾ cup (185 mL) **heavy cream**

½ tsp (2.5 mL) **kosher salt**

Combine the brown sugar and butter in a medium saucepan, and heat until the butter has melted and the mixture is bubbling.

Slowly pour in the cream, taking care not to burn yourself, as the mixture will bubble. Add the salt and bring to a boil over medium-high heat. Boil for 5 minutes to reduce slightly, stirring occasionally.

Store in the fridge for up to a week.

The panna cotta needs to chill for at least twenty-four hours, so start this a day ahead. The recipe calls for 4-inch (10 cm) dome-shaped silicone molds, but you can also use ramekins or any nice glass serving dishes and you won't need to do any unmolding. You'll also need a round cookie cutter, for cutting the shortbread dough to the same size as your panna cotta.

Dulcey panna cotta — vanilla shortbread and blueberry compote

2 sheets gelatin

15 oz (425 g) **Valrhona Dulcey chocolate (or other good-quality 33% white chocolate)** (or 2 ½ cups/625 mL chips)

1 cup (250 mL) **whole milk**

1 cup (250 mL) **heavy cream**

Vanilla Shortbread *facing page*

Blueberry Compote *facing page*

Fresh basil leaves, for garnish

Equipment: Six 4-inch (10 cm) **dome-shaped silicone molds, or ramekins (any size)**

Place the gelatin sheets in a small bowl with cold water, and rehydrate for 5 minutes.

If the chocolate is a solid block, chop into small pieces. Place the pieces or chips in a medium bowl.

Bring the milk to a boil in a medium saucepan. Take the saucepan off the heat. Add the rehydrated gelatin sheets, and stir until dissolved.

Pour this mixture over the chocolate, and mix with a silicone rubber spatula until fully melted.

Add the cream and combine well. Strain through a fine-meshed sieve into a bowl or measuring jug that has a pouring spout.

Pour into the molds or ramekins, filling each to the top.

Chill in the freezer for at least 24 hours.

Prepare the shortbread and the blueberry compote.

Take the panna cotta out of the freezer. If you used a silicone mould, unmold each one onto a vanilla shortbread. (Skip this step if you used ramekins.) Place in the fridge for 4 hours to defrost the panna cotta.

To serve, carefully transfer the panna cotta and cookie into your serving bowls, and spoon the blueberry compote around. Or place the ramekins on a plate, with the compote on top and the cookie on the side. Garnish with fresh basil.

2 cups (500 mL) **all-purpose flour**

½ lb (220 g) **cold unsalted butter**
(1 cup/250 mL)**, cut into cubes**

¾ cup (185 mL) **icing sugar**

1 tsp (5 mL) **kosher salt**

1 vanilla bean

2 egg yolks

Equipment: Round cookie cutter

(4 inches/10 cm if using a silicone mold for the panna cotta)

In a medium bowl, combine the flour, butter, icing sugar and salt. Scrape the seeds of the vanilla bean into the bowl (see the tip on page 208), and rub the ingredients together by hand.

When the mixture has the consistency of bread crumbs, add the egg yolks, and continue mixing with your hands to form a dough.

Cut out 2 large pieces of parchment paper. Using a rolling pin, roll the dough between the parchment until about ⅛ inch (3 mm) thick. Place on a baking sheet or cutting board, and leave in the fridge for 20 minutes to firm up.

Line one or two 11 × 17-inch (28 × 43 cm) baking sheets with parchment or nonstick silicone mats.

Cut into rounds using the cookie cutter, and transfer to the baking sheet. Return to the fridge for about 10 minutes to firm up (these need to be baked at fridge temperature to keep their shape).

Preheat the oven to 325°F (160°C).

Place the cookies in the oven straight from the fridge. Bake until the edges are golden, 8 to 10 minutes. Transfer to a wire rack, and allow to cool completely. (They shouldn't be at all warm when you place the panna cotta on top.)

¾ cup (185 mL) **blueberry juice**

¾ cup (185 mL) **granulated sugar**

1 tsp (5 mL) **cornstarch**

2 tsp (10 mL) **water**

2 Tbsp (30 mL) **limoncello**

Juice and zest of 1 lemon

3 cups (750 mL) **fresh blueberries**

Combine the blueberry juice and sugar in a medium saucepan, and bring to a boil.

In a small bowl or cup, combine the cornstarch and water. Slowly whisk it into the blueberry juice and boil for 2 minutes.

Turn the heat to low, and add the limoncello, lemon juice and zest and blueberries. Simmer over low heat until the berries are slightly softened but not fully cooked. Remove from the heat and set aside to cool.

Gelato and sorbetto

MAKES 5 CUPS (1.25 L) of each flavour

VANILLA GELATO

3 cups (750 mL) **whole milk**

1 ¼ cups (310 mL) **heavy cream**

2 **vanilla beans**

1 ¼ cups (310 mL) **granulated sugar**

¼ cup (60 mL) **liquid glucose**
see tip on page 210

In a large saucepan, warm the milk and cream. Scrape the seeds of the vanilla beans into the milk, and also add the scraped-out pod.

Whisk in the sugar and liquid glucose, and bring to a boil. Turn off the heat and cover to let it infuse for 15 minutes.

Strain into a bowl or container through a fine-meshed sieve, and chill in the fridge overnight.

Churn in an ice cream machine according to the manufacturer's instructions.

This would go great with any toasted nuts sprinkled on top, or vanilla shortbread or fresh berries.

CHOCOLATE GELATO

½ lb (220 g) **80% dark chocolate**
(or 1 ⅓ cups/330 mL chips)

4 cups (1 L) **whole milk**

3 Tbsp (45 mL) **milk powder**

½ cup (125 mL) **granulated sugar**

¼ cup (60 mL) **glucose powder** *see tip on page 185*

⅓ cup (80 mL) **heavy cream**

Chop the chocolate into small pieces and set aside.

Place the milk in a large saucepan over medium-high heat. When it reaches 77°F (25°C), whisk in the milk powder.

At 85°F (30°C), add the sugar and glucose powder.

At 95°F (35°C), whisk in the cream and the chocolate pieces. Continue whisking until the chocolate is melted and the mixture comes to 185°F (85°C). Remove from the heat, strain into a bowl or container through a fine-meshed sieve and chill in the fridge overnight.

The following day, use an immersion blender to get rid of any lumps that may have formed overnight.

Churn in an ice cream machine according to the manufacturer's instructions.

Traditionally, an Italian gelato is a milk-based ice cream without eggs, and a sorbetto (the Italian word for sorbet) is fruit based and without fat. An ice cream machine is needed for these recipes. These will all keep in the freezer in a tightly sealed container for up to one week.

COCONUT SORBETTO

4 cups (1 L) **canned coconut milk (not light)**
¾ cup (185 mL) **water**
⅓ cup (80 mL) **granulated sugar**
½ cup (125 mL) **glucose powder** *see tip below*
Zest of 2 limes

GLUCOSE POWDER

Glucose powder is also known as corn sugar. You should be able to find it at homebrewing stores or order it online.

Place the coconut milk and water in a large saucepan over medium heat.

When the mixture is warm, add the sugar and glucose powder, and whisk until the temperature reaches 140°F (60°C).

Remove from the heat, and pour into a bowl or container to chill overnight in the fridge.

The following day, add the lime zest and whisk well.

Churn in an ice cream machine according to the manufacturer's instructions.

LEMON AND MINT SORBETTO

1 ¾ cups (435 mL) **granulated sugar**
½ cup (125 mL) **water**
Zest of 3 lemons
4 cups (1 L) **fresh lemon juice**
2 bunches fresh mint

In a large saucepan, bring the sugar and water to a boil. Add the lemon zest, lemon juice and mint leaves, and heat to 140°F (60°C). Turn off the heat, cover and let it infuse for 15 minutes.

Strain through a fine-meshed sieve into a bowl or container, and allow the mixture to chill in the fridge overnight.

Churn in an ice cream machine according to the manufacturer's instructions.

This summer recipe is also good with plums, nectarines and other stone fruit. The vanilla mascarpone is a great alternative to ice cream for serving with stewed fruits or warm desserts.

Grilled peaches with amaretto — caramelized hazelnuts and vanilla mascarpone

SERVES 4

Caramelized Hazelnuts *overleaf*

Vanilla Mascarpone *overleaf*

4 peaches, unpeeled

6 Tbsp (90 mL) **granulated sugar**

1 cup (250 mL) **Vanilla Sugar** *page 202*

½ lb (220 g) **unsalted butter** (1 cup/250 mL)

4 fl oz (120 mL) **amaretto**

Basil leaves and/or lemon zest, for garnish

Caramelize the hazelnuts and prepare the vanilla mascarpone.

Cut the peaches in half and remove the pit. Place the halves in a bowl, toss in the sugar and set aside.

At the restaurant we place the peaches, cut side down, on the wood-fired grill until the sugar starts to caramelize. At home this can be done on a gas or charcoal grill or in a very hot cast-iron grill pan.

Once the peaches are evenly caramelized on the cut side, about 10 minutes, set them aside.

Place ½ cup (125 mL) of the vanilla sugar in an oven-proof frying pan that will fit 4 peach halves, and allow to melt slowly. Using a wooden spoon, slowly stir the sugar until it becomes golden brown.

Turn the heat off, and add ½ cup (125 mL) butter and 2 fl oz (60 mL) amaretto very carefully while stirring. It will be very hot and bubble vigorously, so be careful not to burn yourself.

When the butter has melted, add 4 peach halves to the pan, cut side up, and spoon some of the sauce over each.

Finish cooking the peaches in the pan over the cool side of the grill (or in an oven preheated to 350°F/180°C). The peaches should be soft to the touch but not falling apart.

Repeat with the rest of the peaches in a clean pan.

Peel the peaches if desired. Place the warm peaches on the plates, and spoon some of the sauce on top and around. Spoon some hazelnuts on top of or beside the halves. Neatly place a spoonful of vanilla mascarpone on top of or beside the hazelnuts. Finish with some basil and/or a small amount of lemon zest.

Continued overleaf

CARAMELIZED HAZELNUTS

6 oz (170 g) **whole blanched hazelnuts**
(1 cup/250 mL)

½ cup (125 mL) **granulated sugar**

3 Tbsp (45 mL) **water**

Preheat the oven to 350°F (180°C). Have on hand a nonstick silicone mat or lightly greased baking sheet for cooling the caramelized nuts.

Place the hazelnuts on a small baking sheet, and toast in the oven for 8 minutes or until golden brown. Remove from the oven and set aside.

Place the sugar and water in a small saucepan, and bring to a boil. Allow the water to reduce to create a caramel. After about 5 minutes, it will start to foam on top and become golden brown; add the toasted hazelnuts. Immediately take the pot off the heat, and stir well, being very careful as the mixture will be extremely hot.

Pour the nuts onto the silicone mat or baking sheet, and allow to cool.

Place in a clean tea towel, and crush with a rolling pin into very small pieces.

Store in a sealed container.

VANILLA MASCARPONE

1 cup (250 mL) **mascarpone**

½ vanilla bean

2 Tbsp (30 mL) **icing sugar**

⅓ cup (80 mL) **heavy cream**

Place the mascarpone in the bowl of a stand mixer fitted with a paddle attachment. Scrape the seeds of the vanilla bean into the bowl, add the icing sugar and start mixing on medium speed.

Add the cream very slowly to loosen the mascarpone slightly. Turn the machine off, and scrape down the sides to incorporate any lumps. Continue to whip on medium speed until the mixture increases in volume.

Place in a sealed container and refrigerate until ready to use.

Lemon crema with smoked pistachios

SERVES 6

Smoked Pistachios *overleaf*

Lemon Fluid Gel *below*

2 ¾ cups (685 mL) **heavy cream**

¾ cup (185 mL) **granulated sugar**

Zest of 2 lemons

¼ cup (60 mL) **fresh lemon juice**

Fresh basil leaves, for garnish

Smoke the pistachios, and prepare the lemon gel at least 3 hours before you're planning to serve the crema.

Combine the heavy cream and sugar in a medium saucepan, and bring to a boil. Allow to boil for 3 minutes to slightly reduce.

Add the lemon zest and juice. Mix well, and let stand for 3 minutes to let it infuse.

Pass through a fine-meshed sieve, and pour into serving glasses or dishes.

Chill in the fridge for at least 2 hours to set. (The lemon juice will thicken it a little.)

Fill a piping bag with a ¹⁄₁₆-inch (2 mm) tip or a squeeze bottle with the lemon fluid gel, and pipe dots or long wavy lines on top of the crema.

Place a few spoons of the smoked pistachios around and garnish with the basil.

LEMON FLUID GEL

½ cup (125 mL) **fresh lemon juice**

⅓ cup (80 mL) **granulated sugar**

Zest of 2 lemons

½ tsp (2.5 mL) **agar powder**

Combine all the ingredients in a medium saucepan, and bring to a boil. Boil for 20 seconds and remove from the heat.

Pour into a glass baking dish to cool, then let it set in the fridge for 2 hours (it will become a jelly).

Cut the jelly into pieces with a knife, and then purée in a blender. Pass the purée through a fine-meshed sieve to make a thick sauce.

Store in a sealed container in the fridge for up to 3 days.

Continued overleaf

At CinCin, we smoke nuts by placing them on a shallow, perforated tray covered with aluminum foil over a deeper tray that holds a burning alder log from the fire.

We expose the nuts to the smoke for ten minutes, then remove the log and allow the nuts to cool.

At home, you can use a PolyScience Smoking Gun. Place nuts in a plastic container and seal with plastic wrap (see photo). The recipe also works well without the smoked flavour. Just use the pistachios that you've toasted. You can toast (and smoke) the pistachios up to a week beforehand.

SMOKED PISTACHIOS

1 lb (450 g) **shelled raw pistachios**

¼ cup (60 mL) **unsalted butter**

1 Tbsp (15 mL) **granulated sugar**

1 Tbsp (15 mL) **kosher or smoked salt**

Equipment: PolyScience Smoking Gun

Preheat the oven to 350°F (180°C). Spread the pistachios on a baking sheet, and toast for 8 minutes, or until golden.

Melt the butter in a medium frying pan, and add the toasted pistachios, mixing well until coated. Cool to room temperature. Season with the sugar and salt.

To smoke the pistachios at home, you can use a PolyScience Smoking Gun. Place the toasted pistachios in a deep bowl, and cover tightly with plastic wrap. Have ready some extra plastic wrap. Poke a small hole in the wrap, and insert the smoking gun tube. Using a lighter, burn the smoking chips in the gun while the gun is on. You should start to see smoke filling the bowl. Smoke for 5 minutes. When the bowl is full of smoke, quickly remove the tube from the hole and cover the hole with more plastic wrap. Remove the wrap once the smoke has dissipated, after about 1 hour. Store the smoked pistachios in a container with a tight-fitting lid.

Lemon semolina cake – citrus sorbetto, brown sugar and pine nut crumble

Citrus Sorbetto *overleaf*

Brown Sugar and Pine Nut Crumble *overleaf*

6 eggs

2 cups (500 mL) **extra virgin olive oil**

1 cup (250 mL) **whole milk**

2 cups (500 mL) **granulated sugar**

½ cup (125 mL) **Grand Marnier**

½ cup (125 mL) **limoncello**

Zest of 2 lemons

Zest of 2 oranges

Zest of 2 limes

2 ¼ cups (560 mL) **all-purpose flour**

1 ½ cups (375 mL) **fine semolina flour**

2 tsp (10 mL) **baking powder**

1 tsp (5 mL) **baking soda**

1 tsp (5 mL) **kosher salt**

Lemon Crema *page 189* (optional)

Lemon Fluid Gel *page 189* (optional)

Lemon balm leaves, for garnish

Prepare the sorbetto at least a day before you plan to serve the cake.

Make the crumble.

Preheat the oven to 350°F (180°C). Grease a rimmed 11 × 17-inch (28 × 43 cm) baking sheet (with at least 1-inch/2.5 cm rims) or two 9-inch-square (23 cm square) cake pans, and line with parchment paper.

In a large bowl, whisk together the eggs, olive oil, milk, sugar, Grand Marnier, limoncello and citrus zests.

In a separate bowl, sift the flours, baking powder, baking soda and salt together, and fold this into the wet mixture, mixing well.

Pour evenly onto the prepared baking sheet to about a 1-inch (2.5 cm) thickness. Bake for 20 minutes, or until a toothpick inserted in the centre of the cake comes out clean. Cool in the baking sheet. (Keeps for 3 days in the baking sheet covered with plastic wrap at room temperature.)

To serve, warm large pieces of the cake in the microwave. (The microwave will retain the cake's moisture, while the oven would dry it out.) Cut into 1-inch (2.5 cm) cubes.

Place a spoonful of pine nut crumble on each plate and top with a scoop of citrus sorbetto. Set 4 cubes of cake beside each scoop. Garnish the plate with lemon crema, dabs of lemon fluid gel and lemon balm leaves.

Continued overleaf

CITRUS SORBETTO

2 cups (500 mL) **granulated sugar**

¾ cup (185 mL) **water**

Zest of 3 **lemons or limes**

4 cups (1 L) **fresh lemon or lime juice**

In a large saucepan, bring the sugar and water to a boil.

Add the citrus zest and juice, and heat, stirring occasionally.

When the mixture reaches 140°F (60°C), remove from the heat and allow to cool. Strain through a fine-meshed sieve.

Chill overnight in the fridge.

Churn in an ice cream machine according to the manufacturer's instructions.

Keeps in the freezer in a tightly sealed container for up to 1 week.

BROWN SUGAR AND PINE NUT CRUMBLE

3 ½ oz (100 g) **raw pine nuts** (⅔ cup/160 mL)

1 ¾ cups (435 mL) **all-purpose flour**

¾ cup (185 mL) **packed brown sugar**

½ cup (125 mL) **granulated sugar**

1 tsp (5 mL) **kosher salt**

5 ¼ oz (150 g) **unsalted butter** (½ cup + 3 Tbsp/ 170 mL)

Preheat the oven to 350°F (180°C).

Spread the pine nuts on a small baking sheet, and toast for 5 minutes, or until golden.

Turn the oven down to 325°F (160°C). Line a small baking sheet with parchment paper.

In a medium bowl, combine the flour, sugars and salt. Rub in the butter using your fingertips until the mixture resembles coarse bread crumbs.

Spread the mixture onto the prepared baking sheet, and bake for 4 minutes.

Mix well with a wooden spoon, and return to the oven for another 4 minutes.

Repeat this step twice more, mixing and returning to the oven for a further 4 minutes, for a total baking time of 16 minutes. Cool to room temperature.

Place in a food processor along with the toasted pine nuts, and pulse until fully combined and less coarse.

Lemons and their juice are a kind of miracle food. I never think of a lemon as being just a fruit. Full of vitamin C, lemons are capable, because of their high citric acid content, of acting as an alternative to vinegar in salads and even as a preservative. Lemon can brighten the flavour of many ingredients, and the rind, or zest, can create a nice "pop" in almost any dish.

Lemons entered the West in ancient Roman times. Today, while lemons are grown in many countries, more than half the world's supply is from China, India and Mexico. In Italy, the famous Sorrento lemon is almost 33 percent larger than a regular lemon. With its high oil content in the rind, it is used to make limoncello, the second-most popular liqueur in Italy. Meyer lemons from California are a Sorrento hybrid, containing some mandarin orange.

At CinCin, certain plates, like the grilled branzino, include a fire-grilled lemon. Squeezing the roasted juices onto the fish enhances its pure flavours, accentuating the sea without diminishing the char on the skin.

CORNERSTONE
INGREDIENT

A classic tiramisù consists of ladyfinger sponges soaked in espresso and Marsala and layered with a mascarpone cream, finished with a dusting of cocoa powder. At CinCin our tiramisù is a slightly updated version. We use a white chocolate sponge soaked in a blend of alcohols and layer it in a clear glass with a light mascarpone cream. We finish it with a maple and rum sauce and caramelized cocoa nibs, but you could skip the sauce and finish with cocoa powder (it will be just as good).

CinCin tiramisù

White Chocolate Sponge *below*
Espresso Soak *overleaf*
Mascarpone Cream *overleaf*
Maple and Rum Sauce *overleaf*
Shaved dark chocolate, for finishing
8 to 10 good-quality chocolate wafers, for garnish

Prepare the sponge cake, the soak, the mascarpone cream and the maple and rum sauce.

Cut the sponge to fit inside the bottom of clear serving glasses.

Pour over some of the warm espresso soak, and place in the fridge to set, about 30 minutes.

Add the mascarpone cream on top, and place in the fridge again to set for around 2 hours.

To serve, finish with the maple and rum sauce and some shaved chocolate.

WHITE CHOCOLATE SPONGE

9 oz (250 g) white chocolate (or 1 ½ cups/375 mL chips)
6 oz (170 g) unsalted butter (¾ cup/185 mL), softened
1 ¾ cups (435 mL) granulated sugar (11 oz/310 g)
4 eggs
3 cups (750 mL) all-purpose flour
1 Tbsp (15 mL) baking powder
¾ tsp (4 mL) kosher salt
1 ½ cups (375 mL) whole milk

Preheat the oven to 325°F (160°C). Grease a rimmed 11 × 17-inch (28 × 43 cm) baking sheet, and line it with parchment paper. If the chocolate is a solid block, chop into small pieces.

Place the butter and sugar in the bowl of a stand mixer fitted with the paddle attachment, and cream the butter for about 10 minutes on medium speed.

Begin to melt the white chocolate in a bowl on top of a saucepan with simmering water, or in the microwave in 30-second increments, stirring in between. You want to time this so the chocolate is melted and ready to add as the final ingredient.

Slowly add the eggs to the creamed butter and sugar. Mix for another 3 minutes.

Sift together the flour, baking powder and salt to get rid of any lumps. Reduce the mixing speed to low, and add half of this mixture to the bowl. Once the dry ingredients are fully blended, pour in half of the milk.

Repeat with the rest of the dry ingredients and milk, and mix until fully combined. Lastly, mix in the melted chocolate.

Spread the mixture evenly onto the prepared baking sheet. Bake for 15 minutes, or until a toothpick comes out clean. Cool at room temperature.

ESPRESSO SOAK

1 ⅓ cups (330 mL) **strong-brewed espresso or coffee**

2 fl oz (60 mL) **dark rum**

2 ½ fl oz (75 mL) **Kahlúa**

2 fl oz (60 mL) **Cinzano Rosso (red vermouth)**

½ cup (125 mL) **maple syrup**

¼ tsp (1 mL) **agar powder**

In a saucepan, combine the hot espresso or coffee with the rum, Kahlúa, Cinzano and maple syrup, and warm over medium heat.

When the mixture is warm, add the agar and bring to a boil. Boil for 15 seconds.

Remove from the heat and set aside.

MASCARPONE CREAM

1 ½ cups (375 mL) **whole milk**

1 ½ cups (375 mL) **heavy cream**

½ cup (125 mL) **whole espresso beans**

6 **egg yolks**

⅓ cup (80 mL) **granulated sugar**

2 ½ **sheets gelatin**

2 ½ cups (625 mL) **mascarpone**

You can use the egg whites left over from the mascarpone cream to make macarons or meringues.

Place the milk, cream and espresso beans in a medium saucepan over medium-high heat.

In a medium bowl, whisk the yolks with the sugar and set aside.

Place the gelatin sheets in a small bowl with some cold water, and rehydrate for 5 minutes.

When the milk mixture comes to a boil, lower the heat to medium, and pour half the mixture into the yolks and sugar. Combine well with a whisk.

Pour the yolk mixture into the pot. Stirring constantly with a silicone rubber spatula, heat until the anglaise reaches 185°F (85°C).

Strain through a fine-meshed sieve into a clean bowl. Add the soaked gelatin sheets and mix well. Cool to 104°F (40°C).

Add the mascarpone, mixing well with an immersion blender until very smooth. Set aside in the fridge.

MAPLE AND RUM SAUCE

2 cups (500 mL) **maple syrup**

3 fl oz (90 mL) **dark rum**

2 cups (500 mL) **water**

1 ½ tsp (7.5 mL) **agar powder**

Combine the maple syrup and rum in small bowl, and warm them in the microwave.

In a medium saucepan, bring the water and agar powder to a boil. Turn off the heat, add the warm maple syrup and transfer the mixture into a medium bowl. Cool for 2 hours in the fridge. Once set, it should be the texture of firm jelly.

Place in a blender and blend until smooth. Pass through a fine-meshed strainer and set aside.

Best to use fresh rhubarb for this, but you can use frozen in a pinch. You can also replace the rhubarb with other fresh, seasonal fruits such as berries, peaches, or winter apples and pears. Start the preparation early, as the ginger cream needs four hours in the fridge before serving and the tuile batter needs to be firm before baking. You will need a 2-inch (5 cm) metal cannoli tube for shaping the just-baked cannoli.

Rhubarb and ginger cannoli

MAKES 12 CANNOLI

Ginger Cream *overleaf*

Rhubarb Compote *overleaf*

Ginger and Brown Sugar Crumble *overleaf*

2 cups (500 mL) **icing sugar**

½ cup (125 mL) **all-purpose flour**

½ cup (125 mL) **fresh orange juice**

2 Tbsp (30 mL) **melted unsalted butter**

Equipment: One 2-inch (5 cm) **metal cannoli tube**

Prepare the ginger cream (which needs 4 hours of chilling in the fridge), the rhubarb compote and the crumble.

For the cannoli, in a medium bowl, whisk together the icing sugar, flour and orange juice until smooth. Add the butter and whisk until combined.

Place in the fridge for about 4 hours to firm up. (Keeps up to 3 days in a sealed container.)

Preheat the oven to 350°F (180°C).

Using a small palette knife, spread the cannoli dough onto a nonstick silicone mat (placed in a baking sheet) into 12 coaster-sized rounds or 2 ½-inch (6 cm) squares. The cannoli will spread slightly when they bake.

Bake for about 4 minutes, or until slightly golden.

Working quickly with 1 cannoli at a time, use the palette knife to remove the cannoli from the mat and quickly wrap it around the 2-inch (5 cm) metal tube. Use a cloth to remove the tube from the cannoli. Place upright to cool.

Whisk the ginger cream until it resembles whipped cream.

Place the cannoli on your serving plate. Using a spoon or a piping bag, fill to one-third full with the ginger cream. Place the rhubarb compote in the middle and finish with more ginger cream.

Finish with a sprinkle of the ginger and brown sugar crumble. *Continued overleaf*

6 oz (170 g) **white chocolate**
(or 1 cup/250 mL chips)

1 cup + 1 ½ cups (250 mL + 375 mL)
heavy cream, divided

¼ cup (60 mL) **granulated sugar**

2 Tbsp (30 mL) **freshly grated ginger**

If the chocolate is in a chunk, break it into small pieces. Place the pieces or chips in a medium bowl.

In a small saucepan, combine 1 cup (250 mL) of the cream with the sugar and ginger, and bring to a boil. Turn off the heat, cover and let it infuse for 10 minutes.

Turn the heat back on for the cream mixture. When it comes to a boil, strain it through a fine-meshed sieve into the bowl over the chocolate, mixing with a silicone rubber spatula to melt the chocolate.

When the chocolate is melted, slowly add the remaining 1 ½ cups (375 mL) of cream, mixing constantly until combined so the chocolate doesn't set unevenly.

Cover and chill in the fridge for at least 4 hours.

RHUBARB COMPOTE

2 lbs (900 g) **fresh rhubarb**

1 ¼ cups (310 mL) **granulated sugar,
plus more to taste**

1 vanilla bean

Dice the rhubarb into ½-inch (1 cm) pieces.

In a heavy-bottomed pot over low heat, combine the rhubarb with the sugar, and scrape in the seeds of the vanilla bean. Cook until the rhubarb softens slightly and starts to fall apart.

Remove from the heat and taste. If necessary, cut the sourness with a small amount of additional sugar to your taste.

Once you are happy with the flavour, chill to fridge temperature.

GINGER AND BROWN SUGAR CRUMBLE

⅓ cup (80 mL) **packed brown sugar**

½ cup (125 mL) **granulated sugar**

1 ¼ cups (310 mL) **all-purpose flour**

½ tsp (2.5 mL) **ground ginger**

5 ¼ oz (150 g) **cold unsalted butter**
(½ cup + 3 Tbsp/170 mL), **cut into pieces**

Preheat the oven to 325°F (160°C). Line an 11 × 17-inch (28 × 43 cm) baking sheet with parchment paper.

In a medium bowl, combine the sugars, flour and ground ginger. Using your hands, rub the butter in until the mixture resembles coarse bread crumbs.

Spread onto the prepared baking sheet and bake for 4 minutes.

Mix well with a wooden spoon and return to the oven for another 4 minutes.

Repeat twice more for a total baking time of 16 minutes.

Cool to room temperature.

Vanilla panna cotta — strawberries with balsamic and olive oil

SERVES 8

Vanilla Sugar *overleaf*

Strawberry Sorbetto *overleaf*

Strawberry and Cocoa Nib Tuiles *overleaf*

3 ½ sheets gelatin

4 cups (1 L) **heavy cream**

1 vanilla bean

¾ cup (185 mL) **whole milk**

½ cup (125 mL) **granulated sugar**

Strawberries with Balsamic and Olive Oil *overleaf*

Fresh basil leaves, for garnish

Equipment: Eight 2-inch (5 cm) **cylindrical metal molds**

At least 2 days before serving, make the vanilla sugar (for the strawberries). At least a day before serving, start the sorbet, as it needs to chill overnight before churning.

Make the tuiles.

For the panna cotta, place the gelatin in a small bowl with some cold water, and rehydrate for at least 5 minutes. (You can set this aside while doing the next steps.)

In a medium saucepan, pour in the cream, and scrape in the seeds from the vanilla bean (see the tip on page 208). Add the scraped-out pod, and bring to a boil. Reduce over medium heat by half (around 20 minutes).

Have ready a bowl of ice that can fit a medium bowl on top.

In a second medium saucepan, combine the milk and sugar, and pour in the reduced vanilla cream. Bring to a boil, remove from the heat and add the rehydrated gelatin.

Into the bowl that can sit on the ice, strain the cream mixture through a fine-meshed sieve to remove the vanilla bean. Place in the ice bath to cool and thicken slightly. Cooling will ensure that the vanilla is evenly distributed. (If placed into molds when it's hot, the vanilla will sink to the bottom.)

When mixture is cold, pour into the molds or serving glasses, and place in the fridge to set completely, about 2 hours.

In the meantime, prepare the strawberries with balsamic and olive oil.

If the panna cotta was set in molds, unmold using a cook's blowtorch around the metal, carefully lifting off the mold. Place on serving plates surrounded by the strawberries, leaving a space for a scoop of sorbet. If the panna cotta was set in serving dishes, place the strawberries on top, and a scoop of sorbet on top of the strawberries.

Break the tuile into pieces and arrange on top. Serve garnished with fresh basil leaves. *Continued overleaf*

2 ½ cups (625 mL) **granulated sugar**
(18 oz/500 g)

**5 vanilla beans, split in half lengthwise,
or already scraped-out pods**

In a sealed container, bury the vanilla beans or scraped-out pods in the sugar, and allow it to infuse for at least 2 days before using.

STRAWBERRY SORBETTO

5 cups (1.25 L) **fresh or frozen and thawed
strawberries** (2 ½ lbs/1.1 kg), **hulled**

⅓ cup (80 mL) **granulated sugar**

½ cup (125 mL) **glucose powder**
see tip on page 185

1 cup (250 mL) **water**

Juice of 1 lemon

In a large saucepan over medium heat, combine the strawberries with the sugar, glucose powder and water.

When the strawberries are soft and fully cooked, about 5 minutes, add the lemon juice.

Purée the strawberries in a blender, and pass through a fine-meshed sieve to remove the tiny seeds. Chill in the fridge overnight until completely cold.

Churn in an ice cream machine according to the manufacturer's instructions. Keeps in the freezer in a tightly sealed container for up to 1 week.

STRAWBERRY AND COCOA NIB TUILES

½ cup (125 mL) **puréed strawberries
(blend fresh or frozen berries and strain
through a fine-meshed sieve)**

1 cup (250 mL) **granulated sugar**

½ cup (125 mL) **all-purpose flour**

½ cup (125 mL) **melted unsalted butter**

⅓ cup (80 mL) **cocoa nibs** (1 ½ oz/40 g)

In a small bowl, whisk together the purée, sugar and flour until smooth and well combined.

Whisk in the butter.

Place in the fridge to firm up and cool.

Preheat the oven to 325°F (160°C). Line a baking sheet with a nonstick silicone mat.

Spread ¼ cup (60 mL) portions of the mixture onto the mat in a layer about ⅛ inch (3 mm) thick. (You'll make 2 or 3 tuiles, but only be using 1 for the final dessert.) Sprinkle with cocoa nibs.

Bake for about 4 to 5 minutes. The mixture will bubble while baking and settle once it's nearly done. Take out of the oven and allow to cool on the baking sheet. It will crisp as it cools.

STRAWBERRIES WITH
BALSAMIC AND OLIVE OIL

40 fresh strawberries (5 per serving)

Vanilla Sugar *above*

6 Tbsp (90 mL) **extra virgin olive oil**

2 Tbsp (30 mL) **balsamic vinegar**

16 fresh basil leaves (2 per serving)

Wash and hull the strawberries and slice into thin rounds. Place in a bowl and sprinkle lightly with vanilla sugar to coat.

Blend the olive oil and balsamic, and coat the strawberries with this mixture. Add the basil leaves, and leave to marinate for 15 minutes.

You will need pre-made chocolate truffle shells, which come with their own plastic trays. If you can't find them, you can shape the ganache by hand. Pour the ganache into a shallow dish, and place in the fridge to set (ignoring the instructions below for the temperature of the finished ganache). Once set, take equal scoops with a spoon and roll in your hands to form balls. Once all of the truffles are rolled, dip them into the melted chocolate as instructed below. Or simply roll them in cocoa powder.

Chocolate truffles

MAKES 80 TRUFFLES
(40 dark chocolate and 40 salted caramel truffles)

Dark Chocolate Olive Oil Ganache *facing page*

Salted Butter Caramel Ganache *facing page*

80 store-bought chocolate truffle shells (sold in a plastic tray)

7 oz (200 g) **milk and dark chocolate (kept separate), for sealing truffles**

2 cups (500 mL) **cocoa powder, for rolling**

14 oz (400 g) **70% dark chocolate, broken into pieces** (or 2 1/3 cup/580 mL chips), **to coat the truffles**

Make the 2 ganaches, and place them in 2 piping bags with a plain tip that's small enough to fit inside the opening of the truffle shells.

Set out your pre-made chocolate truffle shells in their plastic trays. Fill the shells to the top with the ganache, but don't allow to overflow. Allow to set for 1 hour at room temperature. The ganache should be firm before you seal it.

Melt a small amount of chocolate in the microwave to 90°F (32°C) to seal the truffles—milk chocolate for the salted caramel ganache, and dark chocolate for the dark chocolate ganache.

Place the melted chocolate in a piping bag, and top off the ganache to seal each truffle. Leave it to set at room temperature.

Once completely set, unmold the truffles from their plastic trays.

When you're ready to roll the truffles, place the cocoa powder in a bowl. Have ready a clean, dry baking sheet or tray.

Place the 14 oz (400 g) of chocolate in a microwave-safe bowl. Set the microwave to its lowest setting, and warm the chocolate in small bursts, around 30 seconds at a time, stirring it each time. Once the chocolate is half melted, shorten the microwave time to 10 or 15 seconds and repeat until fully melted and the temperature of the chocolate is around 87°F (31°C).

Roll a small batch of truffles in the chocolate using your hands. Place them in the cocoa powder, and shake the bowl to completely coat.

Transfer to the clean baking sheet. Once the chocolate is set around the truffles, place in a coarse sieve to remove any excess cocoa powder.

Store the finished truffles in a sealed container for up to 2 weeks in a cool place, but never in the fridge.

DARK CHOCOLATE OLIVE OIL GANACHE

7 oz (200 g) **65% dark chocolate**
(or 1 ¼ cup/310 mL chips)

1 cup (250 mL) **heavy cream**

3 Tbsp (45 mL) **unsalted butter, softened**

⅓ cup (80 mL) **extra virgin olive oil**

If the chocolate is a solid block, chop into small pieces. Place the pieces or chips in a medium bowl.

Bring the cream to a boil in a small saucepan, and pour it into the chocolate in 2 separate additions, mixing thoroughly with a wooden spoon after each addition. Once the ganache is smooth, allow to cool.

When the ganache reaches 95°F (35°C), using an immersion blender, blend in the softened butter and olive oil until smooth. The ganache should loosen slightly and become very shiny and smooth.

Allow to cool until the ganache is between 84°F and 88°F (29°C–31°C).

SALTED BUTTER CARAMEL GANACHE

½ cup (125 mL) **heavy cream**

¼ cup (60 mL) **liquid glucose** *see tip on page 210*

½ cup (125 mL) **granulated sugar**

5 oz (140 g) **40% milk chocolate**
(or ²/₃ cup/160 mL chips)

¼ cup (60 mL) **salted butter, softened**

In a small saucepan, bring the cream and liquid glucose to a boil, and set aside.

Place the sugar in another small saucepan over medium-high heat. When it starts to melt, stir slowly with a wooden spoon until it turns golden brown.

Remove from the heat and very slowly add the cream and glucose mixture to the pan. Place the pan back on low heat to melt any hardened sugar.

If the chocolate is a solid block, chop into small pieces. Place the chocolate pieces or chips in a medium mixing bowl.

Strain the hot mixture through a fine-meshed sieve into the bowl of chocolate to remove any undissolved lumps of sugar. Combine well. Once the ganache is smooth, cool to 95°F (35°C).

Blend in the softened butter with an immersion blender. The ganache should loosen slightly and become very shiny and smooth.

When the ganache cools to around 85°F (30°C), you are ready to assemble.

These truffles make great after-dinner treats with coffee. They also make wonderful gifts.

Macarons

Burnt Orange Ganache *overleaf*

Duck Fat Caramel Ganache *overleaf*

2 cups (500 mL) **almond flour**

2 cups (500 mL) **icing sugar**

1 ¼ cups (310 mL) **+ 2 Tbsp** (30 mL) **granulated sugar, divided**

⅓ cup (80 mL) **water**

6 egg whites, divided

1 tsp (5 mL) **powdered food colouring** **(optional)**

At least 24 hours before you plan to assemble the macarons, prepare the 2 ganaches.

Line 3 heavy 11 × 17-inch (28 × 43 cm) baking sheets with nonstick silicone mats or parchment paper.

Place a #9 (⅜-inch/9 mm) plain piping tip into a piping bag ready for piping.

Combine the almond flour and icing sugar in a food processor or blender, and fully mix for 2 minutes.

Pass the mixture through a fine-meshed sieve into a large mixing bowl. (This will help to maintain a smooth shell when the macaron is baked.)

Combine 1 ¼ cups (310 mL) of the granulated sugar with the water in a small saucepan.

Place 3 of the egg whites with the 2 Tbsp (30 mL) of sugar in a very clean and dry bowl of a stand mixer fitted with the whisk attachment, and turn to the lowest speed.

Place the saucepan with the sugar and water over high heat. Bring the mixture to 230°F (110°C). When it reaches this temperature, increase the speed of the stand mixer to medium-high.

When the sugar reaches 242°F (117°C), remove the pot from the heat, and allow the bubbles to settle for 30 seconds.

Increase the stand mixer to high speed so the meringue starts to form stiff peaks. Slowly pour the sugar water into the stand mixer down the side of the bowl.

Add the remaining 3 egg whites to the almond flour and icing sugar, and mix until a paste is formed. This is a good time to add the food colouring, if desired.

Once the meringue has formed stiff peaks and the bowl is only slightly warm to the touch, turn the machine off.

Add one-third of the meringue to the almond mixture, and incorporate well. Add the rest of the meringue, and fold in slowly. Do not overmix, or the macaron will be too runny and will not cook evenly once piped. Keep folding until the mixture is very slightly less aerated.

Drop some of the batter with your spatula from above the bowl to test if it's ready; it should fall flat and smooth after around 30 seconds. Another test for the correct consistency is to place a spoonful onto a plate. If the top is smooth and flat but still holding its shape, it is ready to be piped.

Preheat the oven to 325°F (160°C).

Fill a piping bag one-third full with the mixture. Pipe 1-inch (2.5 cm) rounds onto the prepared trays ¾ inch (2 cm) apart.

Once you've filled up all the trays, let it stand for 10 minutes to form a skin on top. This will help form the shape of the final macarons and the "feet" of the shells.

Bake for 5 minutes, making sure not to open the oven door. Quickly open the oven door and turn the baking sheets 180 degrees. Bake for another 3 minutes.

If the macarons are slightly wet looking or haven't fully risen, give them a few more minutes. Once they come out of the oven, they should collapse slightly and become firm as they cool on the baking sheet.

Once cool, place in the freezer until completely frozen. This will take at least 1 hour.

To assemble the macarons, fill 2 piping bags, again using the #9 (⅜-inch/9 mm) plain piping tip, with the 2 ganaches. Take 1 macaron shell and pipe about 1 tsp (5 mL) of ganache on the bottom side. Take another macaron shell and press the 2 together.

Serve immediately, or keep in the fridge for up to 3 days. You can also store it in the freezer, in a sealed container for up to 2 weeks. *Continued overleaf*

BURNT ORANGE GANACHE

8 oranges

1 lb (450 g) **white chocolate**
(or 3 cups/750 mL chips)

¾ cup (185 mL) **heavy cream**

If you have a charcoal or wood-fired barbecue, place the oranges directly on the coals or in the fire, turning when they are burnt well on one side, about 6 minutes.

Alternatively, preheat a gas grill or cast-iron grill on high until smoking. Cut the oranges in half, and place them on the grill, cut side down, and burn evenly on the cut side only, about 4 minutes. Allow the oranges to cool and juice them.

If the chocolate is a solid block, chop it into small pieces. Place the pieces or chips in a medium bowl.

Combine ¾ cup (185 mL) of the burnt-orange juice with the cream in a small saucepan, and bring to a boil.

Strain the hot liquid through a fine-meshed sieve over the chocolate, mixing well with a silicone rubber spatula to melt the chocolate. Use an immersion blender to combine thoroughly and get rid of any lumps or air bubbles.

Place plastic wrap directly on top of the ganache to stop any condensation from forming on the surface. Allow to |set at room temperature for 24 hours.

DUCK FAT CARAMEL GANACHE

5 oz (140 g) **Valrhona Dulcey chocolate**
(or other good-quality white chocolate)
(or ²/₃ cup/160 mL chips)

1 ¼ cups (310 mL) **heavy cream**

½ cup (125 mL) **liquid glucose** *see tip on page 210*

1 vanilla bean *see tip below*

¾ cup (185 mL) **granulated sugar**

⅓ cup (80 mL) **water**

3 Tbsp (45 mL) **duck fat, room temperature**

REMOVING SEEDS FROM VANILLA BEANS
Vanilla bean pods are used in many CinCin dolci recipes. To use, simply cut the pod in half lengthwise with the sharp tip of a knife. Hold down 1 end of the pod, and scrape out the seeds with the dull side of your knife to use in your recipe. Unless the pods are also used in the recipe, reserve them for another use, such as putting them into a jar of sugar to make vanilla sugar.

If the chocolate is a solid block, chop into small pieces. Place the pieces or chips in a medium bowl, and set aside.

In a small saucepan, combine the cream and glucose, and scrape in the seeds of the vanilla bean. Heat to boiling, and then set aside to let it infuse.

In a medium saucepan, combine the sugar and water, and bring to a boil. Cook and reduce until golden brown and a caramel starts to form.

Turn off the heat, and slowly add the cream mixture to the caramel. Take care not to burn yourself, as the mixture will bubble. Warm the mixture to dissolve any hardened sugar. Strain through a fine-meshed sieve into a measuring jug.

Pour half of the hot liquid on top of the chocolate, and mix well with a silicone rubber spatula to melt. Continue adding the hot liquid, mixing until thoroughly combined.

When the ganache cools to 95°F (35°C), add the duck fat, and thoroughly blend it in using a wooden spoon.

Place plastic wrap directly on top of the ganache to stop any condensation from forming on the surface. Allow to set at room temperature for 24 hours.

Petits fours

CHOCOLATE MARSHMALLOWS

10 sheets gelatin

½ cup (125 mL) + ⅓ cup (80 mL) water, divided

¾ cup (185 mL) granulated sugar

1 cup (250 mL) liquid glucose *see tip overleaf*

5 Tbsp (75 mL) honey (we prefer orange blossom)

2 Tbsp (30 mL) cocoa powder, for the marshmallows

1 cup (250 mL) icing sugar

1 cup (250 mL) cornstarch

1 Tbsp (15 mL) cocoa powder, for coating the marshmallows

Coat (or spray) a 6 × 9-inch (15 × 23 cm) rimmed baking sheet with canola oil, and line with parchment paper.

Soak the gelatin with the ½ cup (125 mL) water, and rehydrate for at least 5 minutes.

In a medium saucepan, bring the ⅓ cup (80 mL) water, sugar, glucose and honey to a boil, and cook to 252°F (122°C) on a sugar thermometer.

Immediately pour into the bowl of a stand mixer fitted with the whisk attachment, and set aside to cool until 212°F (100°C).

Add in the rehydrated gelatin along with the soaking water, and the 2 Tbsp (30 mL) cocoa powder.

Whisk on a high speed until doubled in size, 10 to 15 minutes.

Pour the mixture into the prepared baking sheet, and using an offset cake decorating knife, spread out the mixture and smooth the top.

Spray the top of the marshmallows with canola oil spray, and place another piece of parchment on top.

Allow to set at room temperature for 2 hours.

Once well set, cut into desired size. The marshmallows are ready for coating, but can be kept up to 1 week at room temperature in a sealed container.

For the coating, in a small bowl, combine the icing sugar, cornstarch and cocoa powder with a whisk.

Coat each marshmallow with the powder, passing through a sieve to shake off loose powder.

Stored in a sealed container, this keeps for up to 1 week at room temperature.

We serve these little bite-sized snacks after dinner, but you can serve petits fours anytime—with afternoon tea or even as party favours.

PÂTE DE FRUITS

2 cups (500 mL) **strawberry purée (blend fresh or frozen strawberries and strain through a fine-meshed sieve)**

2 ¾ cups (685 mL) **granulated sugar**

2 ½ tsp (12.5 mL) **powdered apple pectin**

½ cup (125 mL) **liquid glucose**

1 tsp (5 mL) **citric acid**

Granulated sugar, for coating

LIQUID GLUCOSE

You should be able to find liquid glucose (or glucose syrup) at cake-decorating shops and the craft store Michaels. In Vancouver, they have it at Gourmet Warehouse.

Grease the bottom and sides of a rimmed 11 × 17-inch (28 × 43 cm) baking sheet with a very thin coat of canola oil. Line with a sheet of heavy-duty plastic wrap or parchment paper, making it as crease-free as possible.

Place the strawberry purée in a medium saucepan over medium heat.

In a medium bowl, combine the sugar and pectin. Make a well in the centre and add the liquid glucose (the well is to prevent the glucose from sticking to the bowl).

When the strawberry purée comes to a boil, add the sugar mixture and whisk well. Return to a boil and cook, whisking continuously, until the mixture reaches 225°F (107°C). (This can take up to 15 minutes.)

Add the citric acid and mix well.

Quickly pour the mixture into the prepared baking sheet, and leave to set and cool (at least 2 hours).

Unmold the jelly from the baking sheet onto a clean cutting board. Peel off the plastic. Sprinkle with granulated sugar on both sides.

Cut into 1-inch (2.5 cm) squares or use a metal cookie cutter and cut into rounds. Coat well with more sugar.

Keeps in a sealed container at room temperature for up to a week. *Continued overleaf*

2 oz (60 g) **chopped raw pecans**
(½ cup/125 mL)

12 oz (340 g) **unsalted butter**
(1 ½ cups/375 mL), **softened**

1 cup (250 mL) **icing sugar**

1 tsp (5 mL) **vanilla extract**

3 ⅓ cups (830 mL) **all-purpose flour**

1 tsp (5 mL) **kosher salt**

1 cup (250 mL) **cocoa nibs**

Preheat the oven to 325°F (160°C).

Toast the pecans in the oven for 5 minutes, or until golden. Set aside to cool.

Combine the butter, icing sugar and vanilla in the bowl of a stand mixer fitted with a paddle attachment, and start mixing on medium speed. You'll be creaming the butter for at least 10 minutes.

Sift the flour and the salt together in a medium bowl.

When the butter and sugar are well creamed and the mixture is pale white, turn down to low speed. Add the flour and salt and mix until just combined. Add the cooled pecans and finish mixing.

Divide the dough into 4 equal pieces, and roll into 10-inch (25 cm) logs. Spread the cocoa nibs onto a rimmed baking sheet or tray, and roll the logs in the nibs to completely coat the outside of the dough. Wrap tightly with plastic wrap, and chill in the fridge for at least 30 minutes. You can also store these in the freezer for up to a month.

To bake, preheat the oven to 325°F (160°C). Line an 11 × 17-inch (28 × 43 cm) baking sheet with parchment paper.

Right when you plan to bake the cookies, take the dough out of the fridge. (If the dough is frozen, thaw for 30 minutes). Cut into ½-inch-thick (1 cm) rounds, and place on the prepared baking sheet.

Bake for 7 minutes, or until slightly golden on the bottom.

Cool on the baking sheet.

Store in a sealed container for up to 3 days.

BASICS

SOFFRITTO

Soffritto is a building block for many Italian dishes. It can be added to soups and stews and used with vegetables. It usually consists of tomato, onion and garlic, but can also contain carrots and celery. The vegetables are cooked very slowly over a long period of time, usually in olive oil, to release their natural flavour.

4 cups (1 L) **diced white onions** (1¾ lbs/800 g), ¼-inch (6 mm) **dice**

1 cup (250 mL) **extra virgin olive oil**

Kosher salt

One 14 oz (398 mL) **can peeled San Marzano tomatoes**

½ tsp (2.5 mL) **minced garlic**

Store the soffritto and the oil in the fridge for up to 1 week.

Combine the onions, oil and a pinch of salt in a medium saucepan over low heat.

As soon as the oil starts to simmer, reduce the heat to low. Cook for 2 ½ hours or until the onions are a rich golden brown. The oil should be perfectly clear.

Meanwhile, halve the tomatoes, and carefully remove the seeds by scraping the tomato with the back of your knife. Chop coarsely. Add to the onions and cook for another 2 to 2 ½ hours. When the tomatoes and onions start to fry and separate from the clear oil, turn off the heat and add a pinch of salt and the minced garlic. Let the mixture cool in the pan.

Before using, drain off the oil (which you can use a second time).

PICKLING LIQUID

This pickling liquid is a CinCin standby. We use it to pickle daikon (page 34), romanesco (page 63) and ramps (page 31), and even cherries. It's a great idea to double the recipe and keep it in the fridge for any other vegetables you can think of; it will keep indefinitely in the fridge.

3 cups (750 mL) **water**

1 ½ cups (375 mL) **rice wine vinegar**

½ cup (125 mL) **champagne vinegar**

1 ½ Tbsp (22 mL) **kosher salt**

1 **clove**

½ Tbsp (7.5 mL) **black peppercorns**

½ Tbsp (7.5 mL) **mustard seeds**

¾ cup (185 mL) **granulated sugar**

1 **red jalapeno pepper, left whole**

1-inch (2.5 cm) **piece fresh ginger** (¾ oz/20 g), **peeled and cut into ½-inch** (1 cm) **pieces**

In a large pot, combine all the ingredients. Bring to a boil, remove from the heat and cool completely. Strain.

RISOTTO BASE

In a perfect world, risotto would be cooked from start to finish for each order. However, due to the sheer volume of customers at CinCin, we use what we call a risotto "base"— a quantity of risotto that has been three-quarters cooked. We finish this base simply by adding a little more chicken stock, butter, Parmesan, fresh herbs and any other ingredients that give the risotto a specific flavour. This recipe makes enough for any two risotto recipes in this book (Risotto of Lobster from Nova Scotia, page 94; Green Risotto, page 97; Risotto of Smoked Haida Gwaii Sablefish, page 98; and Risotto of Stinging Nettles, page 100).

MAKES ABOUT 1½ lb (700 g)
recipes in this book call for half this recipe

2 ½ cups (625 mL) **White Chicken Stock** *page 215*
or Vegetable Stock *page 217*

½ small onion, minced

½ clove garlic, minced

2 tsp (10 mL) **neutral oil**
(canola, sunflower, grapeseed)

2 tsp (10 mL) **unsalted butter**

Sea salt

1 ¼ cups (310 mL) **carnaroli rice**
(we prefer Acquerello) (9 oz/250 g)

½ cup (125 mL) **white wine**

Can be stored in the fridge in a sealed container for up to 3 days.

In a medium saucepan, heat the stock, and keep it hot.

In a wide heavy pot, sweat the onion and garlic in the oil and butter until soft and translucent, seasoning with salt as it cooks.

Add the rice, and sweat until it starts to "click," about 1 minute.

Add the white wine and stir. When the wine is completely absorbed, begin adding the stock 1 ladleful at a time. Keep stirring between each addition as the rice absorbs the liquid.

Cook until all the stock is used and the rice is slightly al dente.

If the base isn't being used immediately, spread on an ungreased 11 × 17-inch (28 × 43 cm) baking sheet in a ½-inch (1 cm) layer and cool completely.

MAKING PERFECT RISOTTO

What do I mean when I say wait until the rice "clicks"? Some say it's an old wives' tale, but I think you can hear the rice click or crackle, and that's your cue to add the liquid. We keep the rice al dente because it is going to be finished (cooked a second time), so you don't want to overcook it. You want the rice to remain bright white in the centre.

WHITE CHICKEN STOCK

1 Bouquet Garni *below*

1 large onion

2 stalks celery

1 leek, white part only

2 carrots

5 lbs (2.3 kg) chicken bones, wings, backs
and/or necks

4 whole cloves garlic, unpeeled

1 clove

*Keeps up to 4 days in the fridge in a
sealed container, or can be frozen.*

Prepare the bouquet garni.

Chop the onion, celery, leek and carrots into 1-inch
(2.5 cm) pieces.

Put the chicken bones or wings into a large, heavy-
bottomed stockpot. Cover with twice as much cold
water and bring to a boil, skimming any scum or
foam from the surface.

Add the vegetables, garlic, bouquet garni and clove,
and return to a boil. Skim again and then lower the
heat to a gentle simmer. Cook for 3 hours.

Strain through a double layer of cheesecloth,
discarding the vegetables and bones.

BOUQUET GARNI

*Bouquet garni is a bundle of savoury herbs, usually tied together or enclosed
in a leek leaf or cheesecloth bag. It is used to flavour a soup, stock or stew and
removed at the end of cooking. Many different combinations of herbs can be used,
though some are traditional. This is a bouquet we often use at CinCin.*

5 sprigs Italian (flat-leaf) parsley

4 sprigs fresh thyme

1 fresh or dried bay leaf

5 black peppercorns

2 layers of the green part of a leek

Bundle the parsley, thyme, bay leaf and peppercorns
inside the leek layers, and tie it together using
kitchen twine. You can also bundle all the ingredients
(including the leek) inside a square of cheesecloth,
and tie it together.

REDUCED BROWN CHICKEN STOCK

(Succo)

1 Bouquet Garni *page 215*

5 lbs (2.3 kg) **chicken bones, wings, backs and/or necks**

1 large onion

4 stalks celery

1 leek, both white and green part

2 carrots

1 head garlic, cut through horizontally (cloves kept together and unpeeled)

1 cup (250 mL) **roughly chopped tomatoes** (9 oz/250 g)

1 cup (250 mL) **tomato paste** (½ lb/220 g)

Can be kept in the fridge for 1 week. Can also be frozen and kept indefinitely (you can use ice cube trays).

Prepare the bouquet garni.

Preheat the oven to 425°F (220°C). Preheat a baking sheet that is large enough to hold the bones or wings in a single layer. When the baking sheet is hot, coat with a thin layer of canola oil.

Place the bones on the tray and roast until deep golden, about 1 ½ hours.

Tip the bones into a colander to strain off the excess oil and fat. Put half in a stockpot and half in a large container that will go in the fridge.

Roughly chop the onion, celery, leek and carrots. Reserve half of this to add to the chicken in the stockpot. Add the other half to the container, and store it in the fridge (these will be used the next day).

Cover the bones in the stockpot with twice the volume of water, and bring to a boil, skimming any scum or foam from the surface. Add the chopped vegetables reserved for the stockpot, half the head of garlic, all of the tomatoes, half of the tomato paste and the bouquet garni, and return to a boil. Simmer gently for 4 hours, skimming frequently.

Strain the stock through cheesecloth, and place in the fridge to cool overnight.

When the stock has cooled completely, lift off any fat.

Return the cooled, strained stock to a clean pan and repeat the process with the remaining bones/wings, vegetables, garlic and tomato paste; strain, cool overnight and lift off any fat.

To make the jus, return the "double stock" to a clean pan. Reduce to a sauce consistency—after 1 ½ hours, it should reduce to 2 to 3 cups (500–750 mL).

VEGETABLE STOCK

Use this stock for vegetarian dishes, including vegetable risottos.

1 Bouquet Garni *page 215*

1 leek, white and green part

2 carrots, peeled

1 stalk celery

1 onion

1 head of garlic, cloves separated, unpeeled

¼ lb (110 g) **button mushrooms, cleaned and sliced**

10 cups (2.5 L) **water**

3 cloves

1 medium fresh tomato

Can be kept in a sealed container for up to a week in the fridge.

Prepare the bouquet garni.

Chop the leek, carrots, celery and onion into 1-inch (2.5 cm) pieces. Combine them with the garlic and mushrooms in a large heavy pan over low heat with no oil. Cook gently for about 10 to 15 minutes, stirring frequently, until the vegetables start to release their juices.

Add the water and herbs and bring to a boil. Add the tomato (keep it whole), and simmer for 40 minutes.

Cool completely, and strain through a fine-meshed sieve.

LAMB/DUCK SAUCE

Use lamb bones for a sauce for lamb dishes, and duck bones for duck as well as venison dishes.

1 Bouquet Garni *page 215*

5 lbs (2.3 kg) **bones**
(any kind, cut into 3-inch/8 cm pieces if possible)

1 onion

1 leek, white part only

6 stalks celery

2 carrots, peeled

½ head garlic, cut through horizontally
(cloves kept together and unpeeled)

½ lb (220 g) **fresh tomatoes** (or half a
14 oz/398 mL can)

1 cup (250 mL) **tomato paste** (½ lb/220 g)

Canola oil

Can be stored in the freezer for up to
2 months.

Prepare the bouquet garni.

Preheat the oven to 450°F (230°C). Preheat a baking sheet that is large enough to hold the bones in a single layer. When the tray is hot, coat with a thin layer of canola oil.

Place the bones on the tray, and roast until deep golden, about 1 ½ hours.

Tip the bones into a colander to strain off the excess oil and fat. Put half in a stockpot and half in a large container that will go in the fridge.

Roughly chop the onion, celery, leek and carrots. Reserve half of this to add to the bones in the stockpot. Add the other half to the container, and store it in the fridge (these will be used the next day).

Cover the bones in the stockpot with twice the volume of water, and bring to a boil, skimming any scum or foam from the surface. Add the chopped vegetables reserved for the stockpot, half the head of garlic, all of the tomatoes, half of the tomato paste and the bouquet garni, and return to a boil. Simmer gently for 4 hours, skimming every 30 minutes.

Strain the stock through a fine-meshed sieve and place in the fridge to cool overnight.

When the stock has cooled completely, lift off any fat.

Return the cooled, strained stock to a clean stockpot, and repeat the process with the remaining bones, vegetables, garlic and tomato paste.

Strain the double stock and reduce to a sauce consistency (until it coats the back of a spoon), about 1 ½ hours.

MUSHROOM ESSENCE

This sauce is great with fish dishes such as halibut and ling cod, and a match for chicken as well.

4 cups (1 L) **sliced button mushrooms**

3 shallots, thinly sliced

6 cloves garlic, roughly chopped

½ sprig fresh thyme

About 3 Tbsp (45 mL) **extra virgin olive oil**, to dress vegetables

½ cup (125 mL) **Madeira wine**

About 3 cups (750 mL) **White Chicken Stock**
page 215

Store in a sealed container in the fridge for up to a week.

Preheat the oven to 425°F (220°C).

Spread the mushrooms, shallots, garlic and thyme on an 11 × 17-inch (28 × 43 cm) baking sheet, and dress with enough olive oil to barely coat.

Roast in the oven until deep golden brown, about 18 minutes.

Remove from the oven, and splash the mushrooms with Madeira to help deglaze the baking sheet.

Place the mushrooms, scraping off any brown bits, into a wide sieve to drain off any excess oil.

Place in a large saucepan, and pour over enough stock to cover the mushrooms by ½ inch (1 cm). Cook for 30 minutes at a very gentle simmer (the liquid should be barely moving) to extract the flavour and colour.

Strain the stock into a clean saucepan, discarding the vegetables. Bring to a boil, and reduce to ¾ cup (185 mL), about 30 minutes.

BROWN BUTTER
(Beurre Noisette)

½ lb (220 g) **unsalted butter** (1 cup/250 mL)

Juice of about 1 lemon, to taste

Sea salt, to taste

The butter can be poured into a sealed container and stored in the fridge for up to a month.

Dice the butter into 1 Tbsp (15 mL) pieces.

Heat a large frying pan over medium heat. When it gets hot enough for the butter to immediately sizzle, add 4 pieces and swirl it around to melt. When the butter starts to brown (about 30 to 40 seconds), remove the pan from the heat. Watch constantly, as the butter will burn easily.

While standing back to avoid the sizzle and spit, squeeze some lemon juice into the butter. Add a pinch of salt and check the seasoning. The mixture should be heavily seasoned with a strong citrus flavour. Pour into a sealed container.

Wipe the pan with a paper towel. Repeat the process until all of the butter has been used.

SALSA VERDE

Try to make this at least the day before, and the flavours will have a chance to blend. All of the herb measures are for lightly packed leaves, with the stems removed. You'll find many uses for salsa verde—it works well with lamb, beef and pork.

1 cup (250 mL) **Italian (flat-leaf) parsley leaves**

1 cup (250 mL) **fresh basil leaves**

1 cup (250 mL) **fresh mint leaves**

½ cup (125 mL) **fresh chervil (omit if not available)**

½ cup (125 mL) **chives**

1 Tbsp (15 mL) **fresh thyme leaves**

½ cup (125 mL) **green onions**

¼ cup (60 mL) **capers**

¼ cup (60 mL) **cornichons**

1 ¼ cups (310 mL) **olive oil**

2 Tbsp (30 mL) **fresh lemon juice**

Sea salt and freshly ground black pepper

Keeps up to 10 days in a sealed container in the fridge.

Place all the ingredients except the salt and pepper in a food processor, and blend to a coarse texture. Season with salt and pepper.

BASIL PESTO

1 bunch **fresh basil**

2 ¾ oz (75 g) **freshly grated Parmesan** (¾ cup/185 mL)

1 ¾ oz (50 g) **toasted pine nuts** (1/3 cup/80 mL)

1 clove **garlic**

⅔ cup (160 mL) **olive oil**

Sea salt and freshly ground black pepper

Can be stored in a sealed container in the fridge for a week.

Place the basil, Parmesan, pine nuts and garlic in a blender or food processor, and pulse to a coarse texture. With the machine running at a moderate speed, pour in the olive oil in a slow, steady stream, and blend until fully incorporated. Season with salt and pepper.

BASIL PISTOU

If you don't remove the germ from the centre of the garlic clove, it can start to ferment and cause the pistou to discolour. Simply split the clove in half lengthwise, and use the tip of your knife to remove the small bud or germ (usually green).

MAKES ¾ CUP (185 mL)

2 cloves garlic, split and the germ removed

30 fresh basil leaves

3 ½ oz (100 g) **freshly grated Parmesan** (1 cup/250 mL)

½ cup (125 mL) **olive oil**

Sea salt and freshly ground black pepper

Keeps up to 10 days in a sealed container in the fridge.

Combine the garlic, basil and Parmesan in a blender or food processor, and pulse until coarsely chopped.

With the machine running, slowly pour in the olive oil. Blend to a smooth purée. Season with salt and pepper.

SALMORIGLIO

This dressing is usually served with seafood or grilled and roasted meats. The recipe we use at CinCin is a cross between the classic salmoriglio and chimichurri. Preparing this a day in advance helps the flavours to develop, although you will lose some of the vibrant colour.

MAKES 3 ½ CUPS (875 mL)

1 cup (250 mL) **water**

1 Tbsp (15 mL) **coarse sea salt**

12 cloves garlic, finely minced

1 cup (250 mL) **lightly packed Italian (flat-leaf) parsley leaves (stems removed), finely chopped**

1 cup (250 mL) **lightly packed fresh oregano leaves (stems removed), finely chopped**

2 tsp (10 mL) **dried chili flakes**

¼ cup (60 mL) **red wine vinegar**

2 Tbsp (30 mL) **fresh lemon juice**

½ cup (125 mL) **extra virgin olive oil**

Transfer to a sealed container and store in the fridge for 1 day before use.

In a small saucepan, heat the water and salt and stir until dissolved. Remove from the heat and cool.

In a medium nonreactive bowl, combine the garlic, parsley, oregano and chili flakes. Whisk in the vinegar and the lemon juice, followed by the olive oil, then the cooled salted water.

CLASSIC VINAIGRETTE

MAKES 1¾ CUPS (435 mL)

1¼ cups (310 mL) **extra virgin olive oil**

½ cup (125 mL) **champagne or white wine vinegar**

Sea salt and freshly ground black pepper

Whisk the oil and vinegar together. Season with salt and pepper.

MEYER LEMON VINAIGRETTE

MAKES 1½ CUPS (375 mL)

1 **Meyer lemon, cut into 8 wedges**

2 Tbsp (30 mL) **honey**

2 Tbsp (30 mL) **champagne vinegar**

½ tsp (2.5 mL) **sea salt**

1 cup (250 mL) **grapeseed oil**

Keeps in a sealed container in the fridge for up to a month.

Put the lemon wedges (including the peel and seeds), honey, vinegar and salt into a blender or food processor and purée until smooth.

With the machine running, add the oil in a slow, steady stream, then blend for 1 minute.

Strain through a fine-meshed sieve.

Add water, if necessary, to achieve a pouring consistency. Correct the seasoning with salt.

CHILI OIL

MAKES 2 CUPS (500 mL)

2 cups (500 mL) **extra virgin olive oil**

4 tsp (20 mL) **dried chili flakes**

Can be stored in the fridge for up to a month in a sealed container. (After a month, the chili oil will start to lose the spiciness and flavour.)

Combine the olive oil and chili in a medium saucepan. Place over low heat, and slowly bring the oil to 176°F (80°C).

Remove from the heat, and cool to room temperature. Place in a sealed container.

Before using, strain out the chili flakes.

LEMON OIL

**Rind of 3 lemons, cut into strips
(no white pith, skin only)**

3 Tbsp (45 mL) **fresh lemon juice**

¾ cup (185 mL) **grapeseed oil
(or another neutral oil)**

2 Tbsp (30 mL) **olive oil**

½ tsp (2.5 mL) **sel gris**

Can be stored for up to a month in a
sealed container in the fridge.

Combine all of the ingredients in a blender and purée.
Transfer to a sealed container. Set aside in the fridge
for 2 days.

Strain through cheesecloth.

ORANGE OIL

**Rind of 3 oranges, cut into strips
(no white pith, skin only)**

3 Tbsp (45 mL) **fresh orange juice**

1 cup (250 mL) **grapeseed oil
(or another neutral oil)**

2 Tbsp (30 mL) **olive oil**

½ tsp (2.5 mL) **sel gris or coarse salt**

Can be stored for up to a month in a
sealed container in the fridge.

Combine all of the ingredients in a blender and purée.
Transfer to a sealed container. Refrigerate for 2 days.

On day 3, strain through a cheesecloth.

ACKNOWLEDGEMENTS

I would like to thank the Aquilini family for supporting this book and for their belief in all of us at Toptable Group. Thank you also to the Aquilinis for the seamless transition of ownership, and to Michael Doyle for facilitating that process and providing guidance and encouragement throughout.

Thank you to Jack Evrensel, a visionary, who, many years ago, gave me the opportunity to work for Toptable Group, for sharing his knowledge and enthusiasm and teaching me about hospitality.

Thanks to the Toptable Group head office team: Lynn Gervais, Min Jee, Elizabeth Boey, April Penney and Alex Wilde, without whom I would still be writing recipes.

Thank you to everyone at Figure 1 Publishing. Not just for their expertise and their ability to capture the essence of CinCin Ristorante, but also for teaching me about editing and not just being a chef. Thank you also to Kevin Clark for the photography, and his patience and amazing ability to capture light.

Thank you to all the staff at CinCin, past and present, notably Andrea Alridge and Yvan Burkhalter for their support and skill. Lewis Birch for his contribution to this book. Richard Luxton, Shane Taylor, David Wolowidnyk, Elle Boutilier, Jamie Lauder and Jennifer Katchur for their enthusiasm, knowledge and patience with my bad language.

Thank you to all of the suppliers who turn our vision and dreams into reality, particularly Susan and Mark at Glorious Organics, Gabriel and Katy formerly of Sapo Bravo, Kelsey and Lissa at Solefood and Paul at Hannah Brook.

Thank you to Thierry Busset and all of the staff at Thierry Chocolaterie for providing me with food when I forget to eat and caffeine at the start of the day.

Thanks to Terry Laybourne for introducing me to a world of food and possibility. Pino Posteraro for his passion. Francis Mallmann for coming to Vancouver and touching us all with his acute sense of life, and Jim Tobler for his mastery with words.

Thank you to all the great chefs in the world who provided an influence for myself as a chef and the dishes and recipes in this book. Nobody reinvents the wheel, and the process of creativity is partly built upon study and, dare I say it, a little bit of borrowing.

Thank you to my girlfriend, Gizelle, who has an amazing palate/sense of taste and has been an incredible sounding board throughout the whole process of writing this book. Finally thank you to my parents who introduced me to good food at an early age and taught me how to eat. I hope to do the same for my daughter, Molly. My mother was an incredible cook. I can still see and smell the bread dough proofing in the airing cupboard at 14 Drumoyne Close.

INDEX

Page numbers in italics refer to photos. Page numbers in bold refer to cornerstone ingredients.

Andrew Richardson is executive chef at CinCin Ristorante in Vancouver, Canada. One of the country's finest chefs, Richardson hails from Newcastle, England, and graduated from Manchester Metropolitan University with a Bachelor of Science with honours in Hotel and Catering Management.

He began his cooking career as sous chef under Chef Terence Laybourne at the Michelin-starred 21 Queen Street in Newcastle, and later as head chef at sister restaurant Brasserie 21, which received the Michelin Bib Gourmand rating.

Andrew moved to Vancouver in 1999 and was actively involved in the opening of Cioppino's as executive sous chef. He further honed his skills at West, Sooke Harbour House, the Carter House Inn in northern California and Whistler's Araxi. He performed an extended stage at The French Laundry, then moved to Calgary to open the top-rated Blink as part owner before returning to Vancouver in 2012 to become executive chef at CinCin.